WAITING

FINDING HOPE WHEN GOD SEEMS SILENT

Ben Patterson

Calvary Alliance Church
715 - 20th Avenue N. W.
MINOT, NORTH DAKOTA 58701
"What You've Been Looking For"
Ph. 852-0670

INTERVARSITY PRESS
DOWNERS GROVE, ILLINOIS 60515

InterVarsity Press is the book-publishing division of InterVarsity Christian Fellowship, a student movement active on campus at hundreds of universities, colleges and schools of nursing. For information about local and regional activities, write Public Relations Dept., InterVarsity Christian Fellowship, 6400 Schroeder Rd., P.O. Box 7895, Madison, WI 53707-7895.

Distributed in Canada through InterVarsity Press, 860 Denison St., Unit 3, Markham, Ontario L3R 4H1, Canada.

ISBN 0-8308-1727-1

Printed in the United States of America

Library of Congress Cataloging-in-Publication Data

Patterson, Ben, 1942-
    Waiting: finding hope when God seems silent/Ben Patterson.
      p.   cm.
    ISBN 0-8308-1727-1
     1. Hope—Religious aspects—Christianity. 2. Patience—religious
aspects—Christianity. 3. Abraham (Biblical patriarch) 4. Job
(Biblical figure) I. Title.
BV4638.P37 1989
248.4—dc20   89-15342
                                      CIP

16	15	14	13	12	11	10	9	8	7	6	5	4	3	2
99	98	97	96	95	94	93	92	91	90					

To my children—
Danny, Joel, Andy, Mary—
four who humble me
and fill me with hope.

*S*econd only to suffering, waiting may be the greatest teacher and trainer in godliness, maturity, and genuine spirituality most of us ever encounter.

—*Richard Hendrix*[1]

INTRODUCTION
Why Wait?

I hate to wait. My image of hell is an eternity of standing in line, waiting in the lobby of some Kafkaesque bureaucracy. My teeth clench, my blood pressure rises, my field of vision narrows and my temper erupts. I've embarrassed my wife, my friends and myself at things I've said and done when I've had to wait. And I'm forced to do it several times a week—at supermarket check-out counters, in freeway traffic snarls, at the bank, and in fast-food drive-throughs. These daily waits never fail to try my nerves.

But there is another, more acute kind of waiting—the waiting of a childless couple for a child; the waiting of a single person for marriage or whatever is next; the waiting of the chronically ill for health or death; the waiting of the emotionally scarred for peace; the waiting of men and women in dead-end careers for a breakthrough; the waiting of unhappy marriages for relief or redemption or escape; the waiting of students to get on with life; the waiting of the lonely to belong.

For Christians caught in these kinds of waitings, the question is, "How long, O Lord?" How long, indeed. It's a good question, a biblical question. Even martyred saints, standing in the presence of God in heaven, ask it (Rev 6:10; see also Ps 119:84). And it has little to do with how many weeks or years remain. It has everything to do with hope. It's really asking: "Can I trust you, God? Is there any meaning in all this? Why me? How much more do you think I can stand? What are you doing, Lord?"

The great nineteenth-century preacher Phillips Brooks was renowned for his gentle spirit and enormous patience. But one day a friend walked into his study and found him pacing back and forth, terribly agitated. He was shocked.

"Dr. Brooks! What on earth is the matter?" he asked.

"I'm in a hurry," he said, "but God is not!"

Isn't that the way it so often seems to be with God? You desperately want something that you don't have, something apparently legitimate and worthwhile. And you're forced to wait for it. There's no end in sight, and the pain becomes a dull, daily ache. And you can do nothing without thinking of what you are waiting for. Do you ever think that God is taking his own sweet time with you?

Sometimes my whole family is sitting at the dinner table, ravenously hungry, and we are waiting for one child to finish washing up so we can say the blessing and begin eating. Then we hear him in the bathroom, singing idly, the water running in the sink as he dawdles his way to the kitchen, oblivious to our needs. Sometimes as I have waited I have felt that God is that way—distracted and preoccupied and so wrapped up in his own affairs that he has forgotten about mine.

As Important as the Things We Wait for . . .

I write this book out of one central conviction: that at least as important as the things we wait for is the work God wants to do in us as we wait. The apostle Paul says we Christians are people who "rejoice in the hope of the glory of God" (Rom 5:2). Amazingly, the "glory of God" he refers to is the people we will have become when Christ returns, for it is God's good pleasure to one day reveal his glory in us. In fact, the pains of waiting are really the pangs of childbirth—our birth (Rom 8:18-23). Paul says we can therefore even rejoice in our sufferings, the things we must put up with as we wait, "because we know that suffering produces perseverance; perseverance, character; and character, hope" (Rom 5:3,4). In other words, God is doing a good work in us as we wait, producing in us things like perseverance and character and hope (see Jas 1:4).

The apostle Peter is more colorful. He compares our faith to gold that must be purified by fire. As we wait we suffer, but this happens so that our "faith—of greater worth than gold, which perishes even though refined by fire—may be proved genuine and may result in praise, glory and honor when Jesus Christ is revealed" (1 Pet 1:7). Gold refined by fire: that's what the waiting is about.

Picture a blazing hot forge and a piece of gold thrust into it to be heated until all that is impure and false is burnt out. As it is heated, it is also softened and shaped by the metalworker. Our faith is the gold; our suffering is the fire. The forge is the waiting: it is the tension and longing and, at times, anguish of waiting for God to keep his promises.

It is also the way God makes our character pure and shapes us into the people he wants us to be. I saw a man wearing a button which said, "Please be patient: God isn't finished with me yet." God asks the same of us—to be patient with him until he finishes with us. Waiting is not just the thing we have to do until we get what we hope for. Waiting is part of the process of becoming what we hope for.

Humility

To wait with grace requires two cardinal virtues: humility and hope. Humility comes from being very clear on the fact that God is God and we are merely his creatures. We are his beloved creatures, the crown of his creation, but we are still just creatures. Humility recognizes that we exist for God's sake, not he for ours. "From him and through him and to him are all things" (Rom 11:36). Only the humble can wait with grace, for only the humble know they have no demands they can lay on God and his world. Only they know life is a gift, not a right. Being humble is not the same as having a low self-esteem. On the contrary, it is having a sober and clear-headed grasp of the place we occupy in God's world.

Our culture, of course, scorns humility. We are afflicted by what one writer called "instantitis." Whatever we want, we want it now! We believe we have a right to be happy—now! We want our fulfillment to come as fast as a McDonald's hamburger. We value people who "take charge of their lives" and seize life by the throat rather than wait. Not to have to wait is often a sign of success and privilege. Witness the black limousine escorted by the police directly to the entrance of the stadium while the rest of the peons wait; or the diner quietly slipping the maitre d' a twenty-dollar bill to get a good table immediately.

The world is no friend to those who wait. You and I will receive no applause for waiting. Everywhere we are told, in one way or another, to buy now and pay later, be it a car or a house, a vacation or a spouse. We are told that it is not only foolish but unhealthy to discipline our urges and defer our gratification. Nevertheless, humility is essential if we are to wait with grace.

Hope

Hope is also essential to waiting. Why wait unless there is something worth waiting for? There is a logic to the world's frenetic grasping for everything now—not only does it lack humility, but it has given up on a future that is anything more than an extension of the present. Eternity is a vague unknown; the here and now is what is substantial. The world reasons that since there is no great eternal hope to wait for, why wait for anything else?

Christians are hard hit by this attitude. I know many believers who formally subscribe to the doctrines of hope and heaven and eternity, but who live practically as though they didn't. When it comes to how they deal with a difficult marriage, failing health or a bleak professional situation, they live as though there were no tomorrow that shines with God's promises. They act as though there were only the here and now, and they grab for as much of it as they can get.

We need to be reminded of why we may, and indeed must, wait in humility and hope. Together we will look at the lives of two men who had to wait—Job and Abraham. Together they provide a kind of "Exhibit A" of waiting at its best and worst. Job's great struggle is with humility; Abraham's, with hope. We will search for clues in their experiences of waiting to learn better how we should and shouldn't wait.

We won't find anything like "Ten Easy Steps to Better Waiting." There are no "steps" as such, and it is anything but easy to learn to wait. To promise an easy solution would fly in the face of what this book acknowledges: waiting is difficult. It requires an attitude of humility and hope that few of us come by naturally. And so we must cultivate that perspective. If we are going to learn to wait, then we must . . . wait.

When it comes to living, Søren Kierkegaard said most of us are like the schoolboy who stole his teacher's answer sheet before a math exam. His aim was to memorize the answers for each of the problems, score a 100% on the exam, and get an "A" in the course. But answers acquired that way are no answers at all, except in a technical sense. To truly have the answers, said Kierkegaard, we must first work through the problems.[2]

The Bible is full of answers to the problems and conundrums of life's waitings. But they are useless unless we have first worked through the problems. Let this book be an extended exercise in working through the problems of waiting—so that you may truly find the answers to your waiting.

Notes

[1] Quoted in *Leadership Journal*, Summer 1986, p. 59.
[2] Walter Lowrie, trans., *Attack on Christendom* (Boston: Beacon Press, 1956).

I *winced in pain as I looked at my bloodied knuckles.*
In a rage, I had slammed my fist into the dashboard of my
Volkswagen as I drove home from our last date together.
"Five years!" I screamed into the headlining of the automobile. That's how long I had dated her, waiting and hoping
that one day we would be married. Now it was over. Nothing was working as it should. God had reneged on the
contract: I had been a faithful Christian, a good student, a
hard worker; I was upstanding, moral and sincere; I had
loved her long and well—but none of that got me the girl
of my dreams. I had kept all the rules, I had held up my
end of the bargain—why hadn't he? I had waited for so
long!

And now I'd have to wait some more.

CHAPTER ONE
Naked I Came, Naked I Shall Depart

——JOB 1——

When Ernest Hemingway was wounded in the First World War, doctors picked 237 pieces of shrapnel out of his body. As might be expected, he never forgot that experience. But it was not so much the memory of the pain that stayed with him, it was how close he had come to death. He felt that it set him apart from the rest of the human race for the remainder of his life. He recalled the men who shared the experience with him in the convalescent hospital, some of them with faces reconstructed, iridescent and shiny from the work of the plastic surgeons. They too were set apart by their brush with death. They too were suspicious of anyone who had not had the same shattering encounter. Other people seemed trivial and shallow by comparison.

From this, Hemingway derived a formula for his novels: Put a good man into a situation where he comes face-to-face with death—in the arena fighting a bull, or in combat. Then you will see him in his truest and deepest dimensions. You will find out just how good he really is. The trial will not make or break him, it will reveal him.

In many ways, the biblical character Job is a hero Hemingway could appreciate. His name has become a synonym for suffering and waiting—he is a man who was tried and tested. He loses everything he holds dear: children, health, wealth, the support of his friends and wife, and apparently the love of the God whom he has loved and trusted for so long. Job's great suffering brings him into a face-to-face encounter with death that few of us will ever have to experience before we die.

In his desolation Job experiences the most acute kind of waiting. Death seems preferable to the life he must now live. Better that he had not been born than to live as he does. How long must he wait for relief?

But more painful is the question "Why?" The great agony of Job, and of all who suffer as Job did, is not the pain of the actual loss, as bad as that may be. It is the apparent meaninglessness of it all—God's silence in the face of suffering. Where is God when we hurt? Why does he let it happen—or worse—make it happen? Job's waiting is a struggle with these most bitter and primal of questions. And it sets forth and clarifies the most basic and critical issues of human existence—who God is and who we are before God. Until we get clear on those issues, our waiting will remain intolerable.

Of what was Job made? What did he do when his life collapsed around him? The Scripture says he "got up and tore his robe and shaved his head. Then he fell to the ground in worship and said: 'Naked I came from my mother's womb, and naked I will depart.

The LORD gave and the LORD has taken away; may the name of the LORD be praised' " (Job 1:20-21). Those few words sum up what this man Job was made of. He had a perspective that held him together when the unthinkable struck.

Naked!

Part of that right perspective was how Job understood himself. He was very clear on who he was before God. When he learned that he was stripped of just about everything that makes for happiness in this life, the first words out of his mouth were, "Naked I came from my mother's womb." Naked! Job was saying, "I had nothing when I arrived on this planet, and I will have nothing when I leave it. Everything I have lost was not in my possession when I was born, and it would not have been in my possession when I die. My nakedness is a dress rehearsal of my death, a remembrance of my birth. In the end it will have gone full circle, and I will be back where I started: naked and helpless, with nothing and no one but God."

Not all of us are as clear as Job. I know of a man who has hanging on the wall of his basement a placard that looks like a dollar bill. Written on it are the words, "If I can't take it with me, I'm not going." But he will go, and he won't take it with him. It is not by accident that death has been portrayed in Western art as the Grim Reaper. Just as the stalks of wheat have no choice and no defense when the blade of the reaper descends upon them, so we ultimately have no choice or defense against death and suffering. But we can attempt to understand it better by seeing it through the eyes of a faithful Job.

What do you hope in? What is the clothing you use to hide the nakedness of your mortality? Your wealth? Job was the wealthiest man of his times. Your intelligence and wisdom? Job was the wisest of his peers. Your youth and health? Job was once young and healthy. Your power? No one stood beside Job in power. Your friends and loved ones? Everyone loved Job. Your moral goodness and faith? Job was unequaled in these. Nothing makes us immune to death and suffering.

Harry Johnson, a schoolteacher in Droylsden, England, won $1.6 million in the soccer lottery. On Christmas of 1979, he was to have retired. When he did, he was going to spend, spend, spend. Two weeks before his retirement, he died of a heart attack—before he had a chance to spend any of the money he had won. One way or another, Harry Johnson's story is everybody's story. Come sooner or come later, we will all be forced to relinquish our hold on our possessions.

The apostle Paul quotes Job when he tells Timothy that "godliness with contentment is great gain. For we brought nothing into the world, and we can take nothing out of it." It's good to be content with what we have, because we'll not be able to keep any of it anyway, says Paul. Better to hold on to what we can hold on to—godliness.

The alternative is pathetic. Paul writes, "People who want to get rich fall into temptation and a trap and into many foolish and harmful desires that plunge men into ruin and destruction. For the love of money is a root of all kinds of evil. Some people, eager for money, have wandered from the faith and pierced themselves with many griefs" (1 Tim 6:9-10).

People who want to get rich are not the realists they pride themselves on being! Their heads are stuck in the sand. They are hiding from life's most basic reality—that they brought nothing into this life and can take nothing out of it. The love of money is a root of all kinds of evil because it signifies our foolish attempts to clothe our nakedness with the illusion of power and autonomy.

Job suffers greatly. But he has not added to his suffering by believing that his rights have been violated, that his loss is a great miscarriage of justice. He knows he has no right to protest losing anything—for nothing he had was his! It is enough simply to suffer loss; that alone is a burden sufficient to tax the strength of the strongest. We make it intolerable when we add to it the weight of resentment and injured pride.

All a Gift

Job had a unique clarity about himself as a human being which was grounded in his perspective on God. He was equally clear about who God is. Of God, he said, "The LORD gave and the LORD has taken away." The children, the house, the health, the wealth—Job knew that all of it had been given to him by God. They were gifts. They were not things he earned for himself or achieved by his own efforts and skill. Comedian Jack Benny made a speech upon receiving an award. He began by saying, "I don't deserve this award. But, then, I have arthritis, and I don't deserve it either." Precisely the point. Jack Benny said more than he knew—and less. We do not put God in our debt when we suffer sorrow and loss. There is nothing we can really lose, because we have nothing!

But few of us are as clear as Job or Jack. When we are suffering, often our first response is anger, fear or bitterness. Devastated by a series of personal crises, Sean Coxe spent his last $300 to visit his father in Florida. Feeling helpless and alone, he wanted nothing more than to be with the man who had so often been able to put life's disasters in perspective when he was a child. Perhaps he could now. On the last evening of his visit, the two men stood at the end of a jetty and watched the sun set into the Gulf of Mexico. Coxe was seething with bitterness. He said, "You know, Dad, if we could take all the great moments we experience in our lifetimes and put them back-to-back, they wouldn't last twenty minutes." Keeping his eyes fixed on the setting sun, his dad responded simply, "Yup." Stunned, Coxe turned to him. His father then looked steadily into his eyes and added softly, with the wisdom of Job, "Precious, aren't they?"[1]

With that perspective, we can express gratitude even from the depths of sorrow. Note that the first thing Job said when he was informed of his losses was not that God had taken from him, but that God had given to him! Job, at the very point where God had taken from him, acknowledged that it was the Lord who had first given what he then took. Job was thankful even in great loss. How could he be bitter at God for removing something that was not his in the first place? He could, however, be thankful that God had once given it. Job's belief that God—even the God who takes—is generous and kind beyond measure imparted to Job an extraordinary grace and poise amidst his suffering and waiting.

There is a very helpful, practical, everyday wisdom in that outlook—not just for acute suffering. We need God's grace even in our minor sufferings. Think of all the things that "set you off" and make you mad. Let me tell you a few of my recurring irritants:

☐ Climbing into the shower to wash my hair, getting thoroughly wet, only to discover that there is no shampoo. My wife, Lauretta (yes, my five-year wait was worth it!), has taken all of the shampoo into the other bathroom. There is no one home to run and get it for me.

☐ Being eighth in line at a supermarket check-out stand, listening to the person up front carry on a leisurely conversation with the checker.

☐ The neighbor's senile old dog they let run loose. He tears apart the trash bags I set out in front of my house each week, foraging for garbage to eat.

☐ The neighbor's cats, generally speaking.

☐ Toothpaste tubes squeezed from the middle.

☐ The waitress who ignores me when I have only a half hour for lunch.

☐ Telephones that ring just as I am walking out the door.

☐ The United States Postal Service.

Of course there can be good reasons for all of these being irritants—and, believe me, I am a master at constructing elaborate rationales for why I am entitled to be upset. But behind them all is the base frustration that they stand between me and my being the happy, fulfilled person I believe I am, by right, supposed to be.

A Right to Happiness?

There is no single area where the faith of the Bible is more sharply at odds with twentieth-century American culture than this. We all seem to believe we have certain rights: the right to be happy; the right to a culturally acceptable standard of living; the right to health and pleasure; the right to a happy marriage and a fulfilling job. But if we are to think as people of the Bible, then we must never think in terms of our rights. We have no rights! We came into this world with nothing and will leave this world with nothing. Whatever we have, we have because God in his grace and generosity has given it to us. When we realize this, there comes into our lives a joyful gratitude for what we do have,

23

and we are freed from resentment and anxiety over what we do not have.[2]

There comes also a sweet poignancy to our appreciation for God's gifts to us. Last week I took a noon run in the December sunshine of Southern California. The grass was a rich green. I could see the San Gabriel Mountains, stark and blue and faintly snowcapped, against the northern sky. I could smell orange blossoms. I could feel the perspiration trickle down my back. My lungs were full and bursting. It was so sensual and exuberant and inexplicable and mysterious and utterly good that I wept with joy. This beauty was not my right, it was a gift.

Last night I sat with my wife in a restaurant. I ate rigatonni paesano: little ridged casings of pasta, cooked in a sauce of sausage, fresh tomatoes and bell peppers. God, it was delicious! That's right—God, it was good. Thank you! I have watched my children wrestle and play and cry and draw spaceships. I have read them stories and tried to answer their questions about God and good and evil. What business do I have in doing all of these remarkable things? What right do I have to them? No business. No right. They are all gifts. I pray that if ever in his infinite wisdom and love God chooses to take them away from me, I will not forget that they were gifts and still be thankful, even though my heart may break with grief.

It takes a radical kind of humility to be set free to wait in the midst of suffering. It is the humility of one who knows that all he or she has ever had and ever will have is a gift from God, and that we have no right to any of the good things of life.

Who's in Charge Here?

Job's heart broke. But out of it came the sweet fragrance of love and gratitude. He remembered his lost children and home and wealth and health and said, in effect, "Thank you." Then he said something that is very difficult for us to understand, but which is nevertheless part of his wisdom—perhaps the most important part. He said, "The *Lord* has taken away." It was not the Sabean marauders who murdered his servants and stole his oxen and donkeys. It was not lightning that destroyed his sheep and shepherds, or Chaldean raiders who wiped out his camels, or a cyclone that killed all of his children. It was the Lord that took them all away. It is not that Job was naive or ignorant of what we call secondary causes. He knew about crime and criminals and what seem to be the arbitrary and remorseless forces of nature. But the God he loved and worshiped was the greatest and most sovereign power in the universe. He was called *El Shaddai,* "the Almighty." Nothing could happen apart from his decree. Nothing. There were no incidents in the universe over which Job's God was not Lord.

There are people for whom Job's trials would present no dilemma spiritually and theologically. A tragedy, yes. An agony, yes. But not a spiritual quandary. The polytheist would have no problem with what happened. His world is filled with many gods, each with its own sphere of influence and power. Some are good and some are bad. From his perspective, the gods of wind and lightning and the Sabeans and Chaldeans had pulled one over on Job. Neither would the fatalist puzzle over the spiritual complications of Job's sufferings. His world is determined by relentless forces that are blind to the sufferings of humans. It is fate, kismet. Similarly, the modern-day materialist or naturalist would not be spiritually troubled by what had happened. For him, the world is a closed system of cause and effect, a machine in which some get hurt and some do not.

Harold Kushner, a rabbi in Massachusetts, watched his three-year-old son Aaron die of progeria, a rare disease in which the victims age rapidly. I cannot begin to feel what the rabbi must have suffered. It set him to thinking of why God, the God he had believed in for so long, could allow such an awful thing to happen to such a good and innocent child. And what about everything else? Auschwitz? Murders? Cancer? World hunger? His conclusions are written in the best seller *When Bad Things Happen to Good People.* They are: God is good and God is compassionate, but not even God can be everywhere at once. The universe in which we live is a random universe. God gives grace and comfort to the suffering, but he can do nothing to prevent their suffering. When it comes to that, all he can do is wring his hands in grief and frustration with the rest of us.

That is not the God of the Bible nor the God of Job! That is why Job's faith, rather than giving him comfort in his loss, instead is the cause of his greatest agony—at least at first. Job loved God and was convinced of his absolute goodness and his absolute power. Job knew he had done nothing to deserve what had happened to him. Then why? To use the words of Archibald MacLeish, from his play *J. B.,* "If God is God He is not good. If God is good he is not God." For Job and the Bible, Harold Kushner's good God is not God. Neither is MacLeish's. Job's faith will survive this great trial, but not without a monumental struggle. We will have to wait to see how and why. Stay tuned.

But for now understand this: despite the crisis in Job's faith over what God has done to him, it is nevertheless God that he sees in all of it, not the blind forces of nature or of fate, or the warring of the gods. That perspective is what will finally overcome the world and all of its evil for Job. The wind and the lightning and the Sabeans and Chaldeans themselves have no power over him, for it is God with whom he must contend.

For you and me, in the final analysis, it is not the cancer that confronts us, or the divorce, or the loss of a job, or nuclear holocaust—it is God. So it was with our Lord Jesus when he was confronted with all of the raw power of Rome. Pontius Pilate demanded of him, "Don't you know that I have the power of life or of death over you?" Jesus, with Job, could say to the man who represented the greatest power on earth, "You would have no power over me unless it were granted to you from above"(Jn 19:10-11).

Do you see the great strength that comes from that phrase "The Lord took"? Whatever evil has come upon you, you need not fear it, for God is the one who is in control even if you cannot see the whys and wherefores. All falls within his providence. In the words of the Heidelberg Catechism, "all things, even health and sickness, come to us, not by chance, but by God's hand." That, says the good catechism, should make us thankful in prosperity, patient in adversity and confident regarding the future.

Worthy to Be Worshiped
I know the questions remain. Why? Why, oh why? Not in the book of Job, indeed nowhere in the entire Bible, is that question answered, at least not in the way it is posed by us. There are answers, as we shall see. But no explanations.

The real issue of the book of Job is whether or not God is worthy to be worshiped. As the narrative opens, it appears that Satan is putting Job on trial. Indeed, when God asks Satan what he thinks of his servant Job, the accuser answers, "Does Job fear

God for nothing? Have you not put a hedge around him and his household and everything he has? You have blessed the work of his hands, so that his flocks and herds are spread throughout the land. But stretch out your hand and strike everything that he has and he will surely curse you to your face" (Job 1:9-11).

"He's a good man only because you've paid him to be good," Satan is saying. "He doesn't love you for yourself, but for what you've done for him. Take it all away, and he'll drop you like a hot potato." Job is indeed on trial, but so is God—more so. Is God worthy to be worshiped even when he does not make us feel good and seems to have disappeared from our lives? Even when we can find nothing to thank him for in our current circum-stances? Job now answers yes; later he will falter on this issue. When God allowed Satan to take everything away from him, the Scripture says Job "fell to the ground in worship and said: 'The LORD gave and the LORD has taken away; may the name of the LORD be praised' " (Job 1:20-21). The reasons for his worship will be clear later.

G. K. Chesterton said, "The *Iliad* is great because all of life is a battle; the *Odyssey* is great because all of life is a journey; the book of Job is great because all of life is a riddle." We will never fully solve the riddle this side of eternity. But for now fix your eyes on this man Job who sits broken and in anguish upon an ash heap on the outpost of humanity. He would not have chosen to be there. Nor would you or I. But there he sits, unwittingly bringing light to every generation. Satan taunted God, "Does Job love you for nothing? Why, you have made it easy for him to love you. He'd be a fool not to! Take away all of the perks and benefits, and he'll spit in your face." Could Satan say the same to God of you or me? Job proved the Accuser wrong and found in God everything he needed, although he waited, in his nakedness, for a vindication that seemed to delay forever. May we also find all we need in Jesus Christ as we endure our waiting.

Notes

1Cited in *Parables, Etc.,* November 1983 (Saratoga, Calif.: Saratoga Press), 5.
2See C. S. Lewis's marvelous essay on this theme: "We Have No Right to Happiness," in Walter Hooper, ed., *God in the Dock* (Grand Rapids, Mich.: Eerdmans, 1970), pp. 317-22.

My *friend has a horror of profanity. It offends him* in every way. But this was a situation that would try the patience of even a . . . Job. Recovering from back surgery, his last shot of codeine wearing off, my friend received a well-meaning visitor into his hospital room. The visitor asked him unceremoniously, "And what has God taught you through this surgery?" Through clenched teeth, my friend moaned, "He has taught me that it hurts like hell to have back surgery!" Sometimes that's all we know about the meaning of our pain.

We'll have to wait to find out the rest.

CHAPTER TWO
With Friends Like These, Who Needs Enemies?

—— JOB 4–25 ——

A man had a consultation with his psychiatrist. For an hour he complained of his severe depression and loneliness as the psychiatrist took notes and asked questions. At the end of the hour, the doctor put down his note pad, cleared his throat and said, "You are a paranoid schizophrenic. You must be hospitalized immediately."

Shocked, the man responded, "I think I want a second opinion."

"OK," said the psychiatrist, "you're ugly too."

Not a very helpful or compassionate response. The psychiatrist seemed eager to add insult to injury and condemn his patient to hospitalization. In the same way, we see that Job's friends pile accusations and judgments on him despite his pain.

When they hear of his calamity, Job's friends come to commiserate—at least at first. For seven days these three friends—Eliphaz, Bildad and Zophar—sit with him, horrified and silent.

Job is stunned. He is dizzy with grief. Life has lost all of its flavor, and if he could he would spit it out of his mouth. He has just cursed the day of his birth and would like nothing better than just to die and to know the peace of oblivion. The physical pain is excruciating, but the pain in his soul is unbearable.

Neither they nor Job speak. What can anyone say about the inexplicable? Plenty, it seems, from what follows after Job breaks the silence with his lament:

> For sighing comes to me instead of food; my groans pour out like water. What I feared has come upon me; what I dreaded has happened to me. I have no peace, no quietness; I have no rest, but only turmoil. (Job 3:24-25)

Job's friends can hardly wait to open their mouths to tell him what they think this tragedy means. Eliphaz is the first. He asks: "If someone ventures a word with you, will you be impatient? But who can keep from speaking?" (Job 4:2). With that, Eliphaz and his companions launch a series of speeches and discourses, charges and countercharges, lectures and debates that will occupy most of the book of Job. The next twenty-two chapters, to be exact.

If his friends are right, things are as bad as they can get for Job. He's not just crazy, he's ugly too; not only has he lost all that is dear to him, but it's all his fault. Is that not the worst nightmare of the sufferer, of the accused? To suffer is one thing, but to know that it could have been avoided if you had made better choices is another. Hell will be filled with those whose great loss is made unbearable by their greater guilt.

One of the hardest things about the suffering of waiting is

answering the question "Why?" The only thing harder than finding the answer may be pseudo-answers—especially if they come
from so-called friends like Job's. Their encounter with Job is a
case study in what not to do for a friend, or for yourself, if you
are waiting and suffering.

Decibels Instead of Dialog

Some have called these exchanges in the book of Job *dialogs*. But
they hardly qualify for that appellation. For in a dialog, one party
listens and responds to the other in terms appropriate to what
that person has just said.

There is none of that in Job's exchanges with his friends. All
that happens is that each party keeps on repeating what he has
already said. All that changes is the volume—it goes up with each
turn. There is no dialog, only decibels. And if Job's sickness and
loss don't kill him, the boredom of listening to his friends might.
Clearly, there was a communication problem going on here.

A woman visited a marriage counselor with a similar (unrec-
ognized) problem. She told him at the outset, "I want to divorce
my husband."

"Do you have grounds?" asked the counselor.

"Why, yes, we have almost one-and-a-half acres," she said, "but
what has that got to do with it?"

"That is not what I meant," said the counselor. "I mean, do you
and your husband have a grudge?"

"No," said the lady, "but we do have a nice carport."

At this the counselor shook his head and said, "I'm sorry,
ma'am, but I cannot see any reason why you and your husband
should get a divorce."

The lady looked at the counselor fiercely and shouted, "It's just that the man can't carry on an intelligent conversation."

That might have been the estimation Job and his friends had of each other at the end of their painful and convoluted conversation. But God's estimation of the words of Eliphaz, Bildad and Zophar is much harsher than that. More than intelligence was lacking in their speeches. At the end of the story, God's judgment is that what they said was folly and error and absolutely offensive to him.

What did they say to Job to receive such a harsh judgment from God? It is all captured in Eliphaz's first statement to Job: "Consider now: Who, being innocent, has ever perished? Where were the upright ever destroyed?" (Job 4:7). In other words, "Think about it, Job. You know God is all-powerful and completely just. You know he rewards the righteous and punishes the wicked. It's all in the Bible! And it's an observable fact of human experience. Put two and two together. Think, Job: you are suffering greatly right now—for what other reason could that possibly be?"

At first, Eliphaz is relatively gentle with his probing. But there can be no mistaking where he and his companions are headed— they are out to prove to Job that he is suffering because he deserves to suffer. Later on, dropping their scalpels to pick up broadswords, they hack away at his integrity, suggesting the specifics as to why Job may be suffering so. Perhaps it is because he robbed a few beggars of the ragged clothes on their backs. Or maybe he refused food to some poor starving derelict, or inadvertently ground into the dust a widow or an orphan or two. Whatever the specifics, they have come to Job to argue that his suffering is a direct result of his sin.

At the end of the book of Job, God roundly condemns Job's friends' point of view. It was not Job who had sinned, but his friends. In one of the marvelous ironic twists of the book, God tells these men who had accused Job of wrongdoing toward God that they, not Job, are the ones who must fear his wrath. In fact, they must go to Job and beg him to pray for them! (Job 42:7-9).

Job's friends sinned against God. But hear me well. They sinned not so much in what they said to Job, for what they said was true, and could be backed with copious quotations from the Bible. For the most part, these men spoke the truth, as far as they went with it. Their observations had the ring of sound doctrine; their theology was solidly biblical. They merely echoed passages like Psalm 37:25 which says, "I was young and now I am old, yet I have never seen the righteous forsaken or their children begging bread." Or Proverbs 12:21: "No harm befalls the righteous, but the wicked have their fill of trouble." The books of Deuteronomy and Psalms and Proverbs are filled with statements like these.

Eliphaz, Bildad and Zophar were not telling Job things he did not already know and could not read in his Bible. Amazingly, Job agrees that God does punish the wicked and reward the righteous. What he cannot buy is the application of those truths to him. But it is not what these friends say about God that causes them to sin—it is the position they maintain as they say it.

They sin against God because they presume to stand in God's place as they speak his truth. Armed with what he has said in the Bible and with what they have observed in nature and human experience, they have before them what they believe to be certain constants about the way God operates. From these bits of information, they can then begin to make deductions about the meaning of events in their own lives and in others' lives.

God in a Manual
We have a wonderful book at home called *Taking Care of Your*

Child. It is written something like an owner's manual for a car. Does your child have chicken pox? If you think he or she does, then turn to page fifty-three and you will have before you a list of the symptoms of chicken pox. Next to the list of symptoms is a simple chart that asks several helpful questions like: *"Are there convulsions, a stiff neck, severe lethargy, or severe headaches?"* If the answer is yes, an arrow points to the right and the emphatic instruction: *See Physician Now.* If the answer is no, the arrow points down to another question: *"Do any of the lesions appear seriously infected?"* If yes, another arrow points to the right and the somewhat less emphatic instruction: *See Physician Today.* Other questions lead to other arrows pointing to instructions like: *Consult Physician by Telephone, Apply Home Treatment,* accompanied by other lists and charts.

This manual on the care of children is a very helpful book. It has taken all of the principles derived from careful scientific investigation of childhood illnesses and child behavior and psychology and summarized it all in manual form for the parent to use as the need arises. It has charts and lists and formulas and laws and principles.

That may be a fine way for a parent to approach the treatment of a sick kid, but it is a terrible and blasphemous way to approach the knowledge of God and his ways. Many people, however, use their Bibles in precisely that way—as owner's manuals on God and his behavior. When that happens, God becomes a mechanism like the human body, a phenomenon to be observed and measured and analyzed and summarized. The moment you or I treat God's book as an owner's manual, we are presuming to own him!

That is exactly how Job's friends perceive their knowledge of God and his ways. They know that God is absolutely powerful and good and just. The Bible says so. Therefore they reason that he would never allow an innocent person to suffer. From that, they then reason that if a person is suffering, then he or she must somehow deserve it. It must be punishment of some kind. The alternatives are unthinkable. For if innocent people are suffering, it can only mean that either God is able to do something about it and won't, or wants to and can't. In one, he is God, but not good; in the other, he is good, but not God.

It's with these neatly packaged thoughts that Eliphaz, Bildad and Zophar come to visit their poor friend Job. They look at his horrible condition—no home, no children, his money gone, his health shot, and open and running sores all over his body—and open their little book about God and turn to the page that has these symptoms listed. All of the little arrows on their chart point to GUILTY. They have got God all figured out, and therefore have got Job's condition pegged.

The only problem with that kind of thinking is that when we get God all figured out he ceases to be God! Instead, what we *think* about him becomes God. We become the god of God. It's that fatal reversal of roles that lies behind so many crises of faith. Tragedy strikes, and suddenly we find ourselves with terminal cancer or without a job or a spouse or facing some other devastatingly painful circumstance. The logic of the situation seems to present an inescapable crisis: either God doesn't exist or doesn't care or is unable to do anything about it. But what is the logical necessity in that? None, unless we have deified our thoughts about God. In other words, if God takes the liberty to be God and to do something that does not fit our system of thought about him, we are presented with two choices: either God is wrong or our system is wrong. Either we are God, or God is God. The crisis comes from choosing the system over God.

"Theology is the study of God and his ways," writes Frederick Buechner. "For all we know, dung beetles may study man and his ways and call it humanology. If so, we would probably be more touched and amused than irritated. One hopes God feels likewise."[1] God is not touched and amused by people who elevate their systems of thought about him to the level of God himself, no matter how good and true the system may be. God is not touched and amused by Job's very correct and orthodox friends. Nor is he with us when we try to confine him to our orthodoxy —even our biblical orthodoxy. Later on, we shall hear God's answer to Job's questions. But at least he has questions. All Job's friends have are answers and conclusions.

That is how they sin against Job. That is also how Job's friends, and we, sin against God. God cannot be reduced to a set of principles and axioms, nor can a person. God is not an abstraction, nor is Job. He is a brokenhearted father and husband, wracked with disease and doubt and grief. He doesn't need their advice and judgment; he needs their compassion. Instead of trying to stand in God's shoes, they should try to stand in Job's shoes for a while. But since Job's friends thought they had God all figured out, they thought they had Job all figured out too. Because of this they are unable to help their friend. He compares their help to a stream that is frozen in the winter and dried up in the summer; no matter what the circumstances, the thirsty are turned away unsatisfied (Job 6:15-17).

The Ministry of Silence
What might these well-meaning but insufferable friends have done differently if they had had a more humble estimation of

their understanding of God and his ways? How might they have been able to help their friend Job if they had not thought they had him and God all figured out? For one thing, they would have been more willing to practice the ministry of silence with their friend. They started out that way. How much better off Job would have been if they had continued!

Albert Einstein was once the featured speaker at a dinner given in his honor at Swarthmore College. When it was time for him to speak, he stood up and told the astonished audience, "Ladies and gentlemen, I am very sorry, but I have nothing to say." And he sat down. A few seconds later, he stood up again and said, "In case I have something to say, I will come back and say it." Six months later, he wired the president of the college with the message: "Now I have something to say." Another dinner was held, and Einstein made a speech.[2]

I have rarely, if ever, had to apologize for things I did not say, but I have often had to apologize for the things I did say. We live in an age of inflated words that have no real currency. And when those speaking are presumptuous in their knowledge of God and you—oh, how inflated their words become! Those who would heal and bring comfort must learn the value of silence with those who need healing. Where God has kept silence, so should we. Silence can say to the person you love, and to God, "I'm sorry. I just do not know why, but I know God does. Be still, and know that he is God" (Ps 46:10).

Think of the times you have needed comfort. How much better would it have been for you if that Christian friend had just kept quiet instead of solemnly urging you to ponder what God must be trying to teach you through your pain!

Silence would have been better than what you got from the

bore who chattered on and on about the weather and the children and the pennant race, anything to avoid acknowledging the sickness or hurt—as though happy thoughts and faith and trust and a sprinkling of pixie dust would make it all go away. And certainly silence would have been more healing to you than the exhortation you received from the television preacher. He told you sickness was never God's will, that it was the work of the devil, and that if only you had enough faith, God would take it all away. And then there's your super-spiritual friend. If only she had just shut up! Instead she droned on and on about how Christ had brought this great pain upon you for a purpose: to use you as an example of faith to others who suffer!

Just Being There . . .

Job's friends, had they been able to enter into the ministry of silence, might have seen what comfort would come to their friend by simply being there with him. During the height of the integration controversy in Alabama, a first-grader went on her first day to a newly integrated school. Her mother worried all day and, when her little girl came home, she asked her anxiously, "How did everything go, honey?"

"Oh, Mother! You know what? A little black girl sat next to me!"

Fearful of trauma of some kind, the mother tried to ask calmly, "And what happened?"

"We were both so scared that we held hands all day."

I'm scared when I enter a hospital or a home where there is great suffering. The persons suffering are scared too. What will happen to them? What can I say? How would I face it if I were in their shoes? Will I one day be in their shoes? The monstrous powers of death and evil are so much bigger than any of us. They terrify and intimidate. We don't need so much to explain them to each other as we do to hold on to each other and to our God when they come.

That, finally, is all God himself assures us of in the here and now of our suffering. He nowhere promises healing in the here and now. He nowhere promises understanding or comprehension of it all in the here and now. He nowhere promises that if you do everything right and keep your nose clean that he will shield you from all evil. What he does promise is the presence of his Spirit to uphold and comfort us. Paul calls him "the Father of compassion and the God of all comfort, who comforts us in all our troubles, so that we can comfort those in any trouble with the comfort we ourselves have received from God" (2 Cor 1:3-4).

The word translated "comfort" is a Greek word which means literally "to come alongside." God always comes alongside us in our waiting and suffering. But it is rarely to explain what is happening to us. Rather, he comes to speak of his love for us, to assure us that he is near and to tell us what he requires of us as we wait and as we hurt.

I went through two broken engagements over a five-year period—same girl, both times. After the second and final break, I went to visit my friend. I was numb and tired of hurting. I felt dead inside. We talked for a while, and when I got up to leave he suggested that we pray together. I prayed first, mumbling to God the best theology I could think of under the circumstances. I then waited for him to begin. Nothing came for a long time. I was about to ask what was wrong when I heard something—a sob. I asked him what was wrong. All he could say was, "It hurts so much."

"What hurts?" I asked.

"What's happened to you, stupid!" he said.

Cliff was weeping for me when I could no longer weep for myself! There have been few times in my life when I have felt as comforted. He was a little bit of the Holy Spirit at that moment as he entered into the places in my heart that I could no longer enter. He gave me no lessons to learn nor points to ponder about the human condition. All he gave was himself, and that was enough. For reasons we can only guess at, God chooses in his infinite wisdom and love not to answer many of our "Why?" questions. But he does always give us his presence. As we suffer and wait it is better to forget about finding out "Why" and instead learn about "Who." For he is the treasure to be found in all that hurts us.

Notes

[1] Frederick Buechner, *Wishful Thinking* (New York: Harper and Row, 1973), p. 91.

[2]Cited in *Parables, Etc.,* April 1983 (Saratoga, Calif.: Saratoga Press), p. 7.

M*y stomach knotted when the call came to rush* to the hospital. It was the second time in four years I had been called to be with this family—for precisely the same reason.

The parents had been awakened by disturbing sounds coming from their six-year-old daughter's bedroom. When they got to her bedside, they found her having seizures. Paramedics were called, she was taken to the emergency room of a nearby hospital, and a few hours later she was pronounced inexplicably dead. Her older sister had died four years before, at the same age, apparently of the same mysterious cause.

Before this family came to my church, they had lost their first-born, a boy, to a rare birth disorder. All three of their children are now dead.

Last month we sat in their family room and talked of all this. They are lovely people: sensitive, thoughtful, quick to laugh, Christian believers. They had been wonderful parents. They have no doubt that their children are now in the arms of their heavenly Father. Their questions have more to do with themselves. Why should they be chosen to bear such a singular burden? What does it mean? How does God expect them to live their lives, now that they have lost their precious children? What is his purpose?

I wait with them for the answers.

CHAPTER THREE
Cosmic Egotism

—— JOB 26–42 ——

Albert Einstein stood for everything the Nazis hated: individualism, innovation, intellectualism and tolerance. His theory of relativity was particularly odious to them. So one hundred Nazi scientists collaborated on a book to disprove it. Their goal was to rid "German physics" of his absurd and insidious "Jewish speculations." But Einstein wasn't ruffled. He said, "Were I wrong, one professor would have been quite enough."[1]

Those in error always turn up the volume and bring in a crowd to establish themselves. Had Job's three friends been correct in their view of why he was suffering, just one would have been quite enough to convince him. They thought he suffered because of sin in his life. But Job was innocent, and all three of them, hammering away at him for twenty-two chapters, cannot persuade him otherwise. It took only one voice to show Job where he was wrong. The voice was God's, and what he did to show Job his error will be the subject of this chapter.

Throughout the book, Job has argued his innocence and demanded that God do right by him. Again and again he has protested the injustice of it all and begged for a hearing from God. The last words Job speaks before God speaks are, "Oh, that I had someone to hear me!" And then, as though he were in a court of law:

> I sign now my defense—let the Almighty answer me; let my accuser put his indictment in writing. . . . I would give him an account of my every step; like a prince I would approach him. (Job 31:35-37)

Job is like pro-golfer Tommy Bolt, who was famed for his terrible temper. After missing six straight putts, he shook his fist at heaven and shouted, "Why don't you come down and fight like a man?"[2] That is how confident Job is that he is right and that God is wrong. As we shall see, Job is right on the first count: he is righteous. God will never call that into question. But he is wrong on the second: that God has denied him justice.

A New Charge

Now it is God's turn to speak—almost. Before he speaks, a fourth man steps forward to make his case against Job. Younger than Job's other three friends, he has stood on the edge of the group and listened, waiting for his elders to finish their speeches. His name is Elihu, and his harsh, astringent words to Job make him a kind of John the Baptist, preparing the way for the Lord.

Elihu has a new charge to level against Job: It isn't that Job has committed this sin or that sin and is therefore suffering; it is that Job, in his suffering, has sought to justify himself instead of God

(Job 32:2). Job is a good man in the worst sense of the word: morally impeccable, but spiritually proud.[3] Job is right—God is not punishing him for sin, and sometimes the innocent do suffer. But he is rash in his self-defense. He defends his cause at the expense of God's good name. He sets himself up as the judge of the Judge, the god of God, and in effect accuses God of doing evil! For the way he talks, he might as well hang out with blasphemers, says Elihu:

> What man is like Job, who drinks scorn like water? He keeps company with evildoers; he associates with wicked men. For he says, "It profits a man nothing when he tries to please God." (Job 34:7-9)

And Elihu isn't just mad at Job for doing this, he's mad at Job's three friends for failing to see what he was doing. John Calvin commented on Elihu's indictment of Job and his friends. He said Job's friends pled a bad case well, and Job pled a good case poorly.[4] The friends, though wrong, argued vigorously and skillfully the case for Job's guilt. Job, though right, argued pridefully and arrogantly the case for his innocence. Both were off the mark, but in radically different ways. But Elihu's greater wrath is reserved for Job. Job is the cosmic egotist! He has the presumption, the breathtaking temerity, to think he knows enough to draw up a case against God! Why, we can no more look upon God and judge him, says Elihu, than we can gaze into the sun.

> Now no one can look at the sun, bright as it is in the skies after the wind has swept them clean. Out of the north he comes in golden splendor; God comes in awesome majesty. The Almighty is beyond our reach and exalted in power; in his justice and great righteousness, he does not oppress. Therefore, men revere him, for does he not have regard for all the wise in

heart? (Job 37:21-24)
Elihu prepares Job well for what God will say.

Immediately after Elihu speaks his last word, and before Job can answer him, God himself speaks. The Scripture says his voice comes out of a storm (Job 38:1). Elihu had imagined his majesty as coming in a storm ("out of the north he comes"), and that's how God descends upon a stunned Job.

His first words to Job are: "Who is this that darkens my counsel with words without knowledge?" (v. 2). In the Bible, God's "counsel" means his design, plan, scheme or purpose in the world. For example, in Isaiah 46:10, God declares his sovereign power and control over the world by saying, "I make known the end from the beginning, from ancient times, what is still to come. I say: My purpose will stand, and I will do all that I please." The same word translated here as "purpose" is the word translated "counsel" in Job. To "darken" God's counsel is to deny that it is there. It is to deny his purpose and control over the world.

What Job has been asserting over and over again is that God has denied him justice, that the world has somehow gone haywire. How else can you explain a good man having such bad things happen to him? How else can you explain the evil in the world? The systematic murder of six million Jews? The premature and painful death of an infant? A vicious earthquake in Armenia? Has not the universe gone awry? Is not this world a place of chaos, of random blessings and cursings? If God is all-powerful, then he cannot be good. If God is good, then he cannot be all-powerful. If God is God, he is not good. If God is good, he is not God. Where is the purpose and the meaning in all this? Where is the design and plan?

Who Is This?

God speaks to the issue immediately. He does so by asking a question that answers itself. He wants to know, "Who is this that makes such accusations?" That is the kind of question the heavy-weight boxing champion of the world would ask me if I stepped into the ring to box a few rounds with him. Who is this, indeed! Nobody! God says, in effect, "Who is this that denies my purpose in the world with his insolent imputations? Who is this that asks such ignorant questions?"

God tells Job to sit up like the man he thinks he is and answer some of his questions. So he wanted to march into God's presence like a prince and present him with his defense, did he? Now is his opportunity. God says to Job, "Brace yourself like a man; I will question you, and you shall answer me" (Job 38:3). What follows is a series of questions in a tone of sustained sarcasm that will systematically dismantle Job's self-confidence. Hear just a few of the first (Job 38:4-6):

☐ Where were you when I laid the earth's foundations?

☐ Who marked off its dimensions? Surely you know! Who stretched a measuring line across it?

☐ On what were its footings set? Who laid its cornerstone?

God has only just begun. The pace quickens as he hurls one question after another at Job: "Have you ever given orders to the morning? Have the gates of death been shown to you? Have you comprehended the vast expanses of the earth? Surely you know. . . . You have lived so many years!" (Job 38:12, 17-18, 21).

Question piles upon question as God asks Job again and again to answer the unanswerable. God seems to get more excited as he leaps from one part of creation to another and asks Job to explain it. It is like, "Have you seen this, Job? Do you understand

51

it? Or how about this? And this? And, oh, have you seen what I did over here?" It doesn't matter where God looks in the world. It can be clouds or stars or lightning or lions or mountain goats or donkeys or the silly and magnificent ostrich. It can be stallions or hawks, alligators or hippopotami. "Did you make these, Job? Can you control them? Can you even begin to comprehend them?"

"You can think of God as a great cosmic bully here if you want," writes Frederick Buechner, "but you can think of him also as a great cosmic artist, a singer, say, of such power and magnif-icence and so caught up in the incandescence of his own art that he never notices that he has long since ruptured the eardrums of his listeners and reduced them to quivering pulp." [5]

In the middle of it all, God pauses to ask Job, "Will the one who contends with the Almighty correct him? Let him who ac-cuses God answer him!" And Job can only respond with, "I am unworthy—how can I reply to you? I put my hand over my mouth. I spoke once, but I have no answer—twice, but I will say no more" (Job 40:1-5). In other words, "I got nothing to say, Lord." But *God* does, and the storm rages unabated as he con-tinues his questioning of Job for yet another two chapters. The point is not lost on Job. When God is finished with his questions, Job is also finished with his. He replies to God:

> I know that you can do all things; no plan of yours can be thwarted. You asked, "Who is this that obscures my counsel without knowledge?" Surely I spoke of things I did not under-stand, things too wonderful for me to know (Job 42:1-3).

Note that God has not attempted to answer any of Job's questions. He barely even acknowledges them. He offers no explanations for his suffering, no theories as to how God's justice and power can coexist in a world filled with evil and injustice. All he does is confront Job with his ignorance, and that is sufficient for Job. He receives it as an answer.

God doesn't even tell him about the exchange between himself and Satan in heaven. Remember, Satan had stood before God in the heavenly court and asserted that Job was a servant of God only because God rewarded his service. Take the rewards away and Job will curse you, said Satan. At one level, Satan's attack was directed at Job and his integrity. But at another, deeper level, it was an attack on the excellence and worthiness of God—that in himself, God wasn't worthy to be worshipped. He has to give Job "reasons" to respect him—that is, rewards and favors for his devotion. As God takes Job on his whirlwind tour of the universe, piling question upon question upon his furrowed brow, he lays that allegation to rest forever.

Cosmic Egotism

What does God do for Job in that brutal interrogation? He shatters his egotism. He slaps him with the limits of his intellect. He demonstrates that the universe he made and manages is wilder and bigger and more terrifying than Job could ever understand. In comparison to the world he created, Job's mind is a fleck of dust on the eyelash of a gnat. "We are the faint tracing on the surface of mystery," writes Annie Dillard.[6] The mystery that is the ground of our being can be approached, but never penetrated. Suffering and evil belong to that mystery. God would relieve Job and you and me of the egotism that thinks we can. Wisdom looks in awe at a universe so immense "the center of which is everywhere, the circumference nowhere,"[7] and bows humbly before the power that can create and administrate such a place.

But Job's egotism is more than intellectual; it is the unique kind of egotism that often comes with great pain. The effect of pain is claustrophobic: it has a way of making the sufferer implode upon himself. The great temptation of suffering is to let your pain become the whole world and to start believing that all that ever was, is and will be, is your private hell. As hard and as brutal as it may seem, God's frontal assault on Job's egotism really liberates him from the notion that his suffering is the whole world. It tells him that there is a great big world out there, a world that is infinitely greater than his suffering.

The first four years of my marriage and ministry were spent in the lovely seaside town of La Jolla, California. Shortly after I joined the staff of the church there, one of the other associate pastors took my wife and me on a drive up a hill that overlooks the ocean. From there the blue sky and sparkling ocean seemed endless. He said, "You know, whenever I am depressed, I drive my car up here and look at this, and when I do, I cannot remain depressed." Many times in the four years I was on the staff of that church I tried his remedy for depression, and it worked every time. It didn't work because that scene's exquisite beauty was a diversion, something to get my mind off my troubles. It worked because it put my problems in their proper context—the vast and spectacular world that is ruled with infinite wisdom by the God and Father of our Lord Jesus Christ. It got me out of myself.

Later on, when I came to the church I now pastor, I experienced a terribly discouraging winter in 1977. I was ready to quit the church. But I remembered what that kind of scene did for me, so I took a short vacation and hiked alone into the Grand Canyon. As I walked I memorized the fortieth chapter of Isaiah, the great hymn of praise to God's sovereign power and wisdom. As I descended into that immense gorge, hiking along its ancient, towering walls, looking down on the mighty Colorado River, looking up at a cobalt sky, words like these were ringing in my mind:

To whom will you compare me? Or who is my equal?" says the Holy One. . . . Why do you say . . . "My way is hidden from the LORD; my cause is disregarded by my God"? Do you not know? Have you not heard? The LORD is the everlasting God, the Creator of the ends of the earth . . . and his understanding no one can fathom. He gives strength to the weary and increases the power of the weak. (Is 40:25-29)

I came back to my ministry ready to press on in the face of my frustrations.

We all can't take trips to the Grand Canyon or to La Jolla when we suffer. But we can let God puncture our egotism and remind us of the bigness of the world he rules with love. The pain may remain, but not as before, for now it will be put in its place. It is enough just to hurt. Our hurt need not bear the burden of being the whole universe. If God can manage a troubled world, he can take care of your world of trouble.

Bruce Larson had an unusual way of convincing people to turn their lives over to Jesus Christ. When he was working in New York City, he would walk a man or woman downtown to the front of the RCA building on Fifth Avenue. In front of the building there is a gigantic statue of a massively proportioned, magnificently muscled Atlas, the world resting on his shoulders. As powerfully built as he is, he is straining under the weight, barely able to stand. Larson would say, "Now that's one way to live, trying to carry the world on your shoulders. But now come across the street with me."

Across the street is St. Patrick's Cathedral. There behind the altar is a little shrine of the boy Jesus. He appears to be no more than eight or nine years old. As little and as frail as he appears, he is holding the world in one hand! Then Larson would say, "We have a choice. We can carry the world on our shoulders, or we can say, 'I give up, Lord; here's my life. I give you my world, the whole world.' "[8]

Wise Agnosticism

With the departure of Job's egotism came a wise agnosticism. He didn't know why everything happened, and he didn't have to know why. All he had to know was who was in control. Job concluded that what puzzled him was no puzzle to God, and that was enough. That is what the word *agnostic* means—one who doesn't know. There are some things in this life—no, many things—that we cannot know, and the sooner we come to terms with that fact, the happier we will be. Usually it is our egotism that feels it must know everything.

There is a story in the Talmud about a wise and pious rabbi named Akiba. He had taken a trip to a strange country where mystery still dwelt. With him he took his three possessions—an ass, a rooster and a lamp. When he stopped at a village for lodging, the people drove him out and he was forced to spend the night in the forest. Being the holy and pious man he was, he took his pains with ease and said, "All that God does is done well."

So he found a tree under which to sleep, lit his lamp and prepared to study the Torah before retiring. But a fierce wind blew out the light, forcing him to go to sleep early. Later that night, wild animals came through and chased away his rooster. Still later, thieves took his ass. But, in each case, Rabbi Akiba said, "All that God does is done well."

56

The next morning he went back to the village. There he discovered that soldiers had come and killed everyone in the village.
Had he been permitted to stay there, he too would have died. He
learned also that the soldiers had traveled through the same part
of the forest where he had slept. Had they seen the light of his
lamp or heard his rooster crow or ass bray, again, he would have
been killed. Thinking on all of these things, he replied as he
always did: "All that God does is done well."

Once in a while we are permitted the perspective on our lives
and our sufferings that was permitted Rabbi Akiba. But usually
not. All we can cling to is that even though we do not know why
God does what he does, he can know that nothing thwarts his
purpose, and that in all things he works for our good (Rom 8:28).

The world we live on is a tiny dot in a fathomless universe.
Each of us is but a tiny speck upon the dot of the earth. Our lives
are but a moment, a breath, a vapor on that planet. We are in-
finitesimally small, and our lives are excruciatingly brief. In any
of our lifetimes, in all of the lifetimes of all of the people of the
earth, we will never know more than one one-millionth of what
is to be known about God and his ways with people.

Thomas Carlyle wrote: "Does the minnow understand the
oceantides and periodic currents, the trade winds and monsoons
and moon's eclipses, by all of which the condition of its little
creek is regulated, and may, from time to time, be quite overset
and reversed? Such a minnow is man; his creek, this planet earth;
his ocean, the immeasurable all; his monsoons and periodic currents, the mysterious course of providence." So let us rest in the
assurance that "all that God does is done well." Let him do his
work.

I will never forget the look of terror and confusion on my

eighteen-month-old son's face as I held him in restraint as a lab technician pricked his little fingers for a blood sample. As he screamed bloody murder, his eyes searched mine for an explanation. Why, this was his daddy! The one who loves him. Why was he letting this happen to him? Why was he apparently making it happen? He could not know. All he could do was cling to me in trust in the midst of his pain and confusion. We serve a God who can be trusted even when his ways transcend our intellects— *especially* when they do.

Humble Clarity

We won't be able to trust this way until we are clear on the place we occupy in the universe. And that kind of clarity can never come until we are convinced that God is indeed God and we are mere creatures; that our thoughts are not his thoughts, nor are our ways his ways; but that as high as the heavens are above the earth, so are his thoughts higher than our thoughts and his ways than our ways (Is 55:8-9). Until we are absolutely clear on that fundamental truth, our imperious egos will forever be clamoring for God to explain himself to us. And if he chooses to remain silent, we will conclude he is incompetent or malevolent or un-caring or simply absent. And our acute, intense waitings will embitter and destroy us.

That clarity is nothing more nor less than the virtue of humility. It is not a low view of oneself, it is simply a clear view of oneself in relation to others and, above all, to God. John Calvin preached 159 sermons from the book of Job. In each, he concluded with these words, or with words very nearly like them: "Now we shall present ourselves before the face of God and bow in humble reverence." Whatever the lesson Calvin the pastor-theologian wanted to draw from a given text in Job, the upshot of it was always to bow in humble reverence before the face of God. I cannot tell you the reason you are waiting and suffering as you are. But I am certain of the response God is seeking from you as you wait—*humble reverence.* Without it, we simply cannot wait in peace and with faith.

The Bible is full of the promises God makes to those who wait for him. We will be considering them on the pages that follow. But until we learn humble reverence, they will be forever beyond our grasp.

Notes

[1]Quoted by Clifton Fadiman, ed., *Little, Brown Book of Anecdotes* (Boston: Little, Brown and Co., 1985), p. 187.

[2]Ibid., p. 69.

[3]A line attributed to Mark Twain.

[4]Cited by Harold Dekker in John Calvin, *Introduction to Sermons From Job,* trans. and ed. Leroy Nixon (Grand Rapids, Mich.: Baker, 1979), p. xxxvi.

[5]Frederick Buechner, *Peculiar Treasures* (New York: Harper and Row, 1979), p.67.

[6]Annie Dillard, *Pilgrim at Tinker Creek* (New York: Harper's Magazine Press, 1974), p.9.

[7]Blaise Pascal, *Pensées* (Chicago: The Great Books, University of Chicago Press, 1952), p. 181.

[8]Bruce Larson, cited in *Leadership Journal* 40 (Winter 1987).

G*wen's eyes twinkled as she told the story. The year* she graduated, she was the youngest woman ever to finish medical college in the British Isles. When she arrived at the mission station in northern India, she felt as if she had finally come home. All she had waited for—all the hard work, all the years in school, all she had pointed toward since she was a girl had come to fruition at last. No more waiting! Now Gwen could begin her life's work. As she walked across the grounds of the station, her heart overflowed with thanksgiving. She prayed, "Thank you, Lord, for bringing me to the place where I will do my life's work."

When God spoke back, she was not as surprised that he spoke as she was by what he said. Said God: "If I tell you to move tomorrow, you'll move!"

It wasn't long before he did, and she did. That was more than forty astonishingly productive and adventure-filled years ago. Gwen's lived all over the world.

The last time I talked to her she was still waiting to come home.

CHAPTER FOUR
Journey on a Promise

—— GENESIS 12:1-9 ——

Abram and Sarai are waiting.

It's been so long. He's seventy-five years old, she's not much younger, and still they are childless. Childlessness was a double agony for these two. There was the sadness and disappointment of having no pink, soft little baby, no childish laughter in the tent, no stories to tell when others talked of their children. Worse, there was the stigma. *Barren* was the word for a childless woman in their culture. Barren! It spoke of emptiness, of shame, of failure to realize one's destiny. Sarai was believed to have failed to do what she was created to do as a woman. Their story begins in the twelfth chapter of Genesis.

The whole creation is waiting too, breathless and aching with suspense. God created a magnificent world, but it is now fractured and fallen because of sin. Through the fall of the first humans, Adam and Eve, the world is spiralling downward to destruction. The first eleven chapters of Genesis read like film footage of a disaster—"a tornado hits the coast with high winds and pelting rain"—recording the devastation of sin. It's as if the creation is caught in a vortex: alienation as Adam and Eve are driven out of the Garden of Eden; murderous hatred as Cain kills his brother Abel; judgment and destruction as a flood destroys the world; and finally, the megalomania and chaos of the Tower of Babel.

A drama with great suspense unfolds: What will God do about all this? Sin continues to wreak its havoc upon the world God created in love. Will he simply let it all fall apart? Or will he act to save it and its people? The whole creation is waiting, in unbearable tension, to see what God will do.

As it turns out, the creation is waiting for the same thing Abram and Sarai are waiting for! To their immense surprise, they discover that their waiting for a child is linked to a much greater Waiting— the Waiting of the world for its redemption. And the fulfillment of Abram and Sarai's waiting will set in motion God's campaign to restore his fallen creation. The birth of a child, their child, will be the vehicle for redemption. God says to Abram:

Leave your country, your people and your father's household
and go to the land that I will show you.
I will make you into a great nation
  and I will bless you;
I will make your name great,
  and you will be a blessing.
I will bless those who bless you,
  and whoever curses you I will curse;
and all peoples on earth

will be blessed through you. (Gen 12:1-3)

A great nation. That's what God will make of Abram as he moves to redeem his world. To become a great nation, Abram and Sarai must have descendants, lots of them! To have lots of descendants, Sarai must become—dare she even say it out loud?—pregnant! In her old age! Not only will they become a great nation, but they will have a great land and a great name and they will be a great blessing to the whole world. That is God's gracious promise to these two waiters.

The Silence of God's Higher Thoughts[1]

Take heart, you who wait! What God did for Abram and Sarai he does for all who wait for him. He is for you, not against you; he feels your ache, he hears your groaning. And note: If he is silent now, as he was for so many years with Abram and Sarai, it is the silence of his higher thoughts. He is up to something so big and so unimaginably good that your mind cannot contain it.

Abram and Sarai received from God so much better than what they wanted. They would have settled for just a baby; what they got was a baby who would be the progenitor of a nation, a baby through whom God would bless the whole world. Through their son, they would become the ancestors of none other than Jesus Christ! All the years they were waiting and wondering if God heard their prayers—and if he did, did he even care?—God was quietly doing a good work for them and for the entire human race that would dwarf, in excellence and beauty, the thing they hoped for. What we see God doing is never as good as what we don't see.

We must learn to place all of our little waitings within the context of a larger Waiting—the Waiting for God's redemption of his fallen creation. The things you and I wait for—a child, a job, health, happiness, fulfillment—these are mere signs and shadows of the redemption that is to come. Whether God grants us our dreams or denies them, he does so only as part of his larger plan to save us for eternity.

In the eighth chapter of the book of Romans, the apostle Paul connects our individual waitings with a great cosmic Waiting. He says the whole "creation itself will be liberated from its bondage to decay" as it is "brought into the glorious freedom of the children of God." The fulfillment of our waitings will mean the fulfillment of its Waiting. Until then, it waits and groans "as in the pains of childbirth," even as we "groan inwardly as we wait eagerly for our . . . redemption." Until then, we can be assured that "in all things God works for the good of those who love him" (Rom 8:21-23, 28).

God's dealings with us are always on the order of what he did with Abram and Sarai. He makes his promises, and he will keep his promises; but just how and when he will keep them is something for which we must wait. But keep them he will, and in ways other and better than we can think, as he works for our good in all things. As he promised to Jeremiah, under the bleakest possible of circumstances, so with us: " 'For I know the plans I have for you,' declares the LORD, 'plans to prosper you and not to harm you, plans to give you a hope and a future' " (Jer 29:11).

God's Initiative with Ordinary People

Reflect for a moment on the grace that makes this kind of promise. It's given entirely on God's own initiative. He makes the first move. There is no mention in the story if Abram and Sarai were even asking anymore for a child. God just does it; he makes the

66

promise gratis, freely and totally unanticipated. That's the way it is with God's grace. That is what grace is by definition—a gift. As Jesus told his disciples: "You did not choose me, but I chose you" (Jn 15:16). This grace was unmerited and unplanned. Paul celebrated the cross of Christ by saying, "But God demonstrates his own love for us in this: While we were still sinners, Christ died for us" (Rom 5:8). Again, grace, gift, gratis: while we were sinners, that is, before we cared and whether or not we ever would, God extended himself to us in love, completely.

For a while I wondered why the wrenching film *Ordinary People* was given that title. If you didn't see it, it is the story of the disintegration of a family in the aftermath of death. The elder and favored of two sons dies in a boating accident. The perfectionist mother cannot fit his death into her compulsively ordered world. The younger son cannot face the guilt he feels because it was he, not his brother, who survived. The father is isolated and impotent as he watches his wife and son slowly crumble. I wondered: What is *ordinary* about these people? They are wealthy, upper-middle class, they live in one of Chicago's finest suburbs, and they are decimated by tragedy.

What made them ordinary, what makes us all ordinary, what puts us all in the same boat with everybody else, rich or poor, high or low, is our inability to stand when life crushes us with its awful weight. The grace of God seen in his promise to Abram and Sarai is that it comes seemingly out of nowhere into ordinary lives, whether those ordinary lives are lived by presidents or professional athletes, by fry cooks or computer programmers. It speaks our names and says, "Come, leave your country and go to the place I will show you, and receive the gift I will give you." He takes the initiative with us.

Oblivious to Character

His promise is grace also because it is given oblivious to Abram's character. Nothing is said, one way or the other, about his moral goodness, or lack thereof. Centuries later, when Moses was explaining to Israel why God delivered them from slavery in Egypt, the only reason he could come up with was this: "Because he *loved* your forefathers" (Deut 4:37, emphasis mine). One can almost hear them saying, "Is that all? Just because he loved us? Not because we were so great and wonderful?" That's right. That's how it is with grace—it is a gift freely given, not payment or tribute or wages. It is given because the giver is wonderful, not because the givee is.

That is definitely not how business is transacted in this world. The Downstown comic strip pictured a department store Santa holding a little boy on his lap. The boy had just given Santa his Christmas list and was asking, "Will I get everything I asked for this Christmas, Santa?"

Santa replied, "That depends on whether or not you are a good boy or a bad boy. By the way, what does your old man do?"

"He's a vice president for General Motors."

Patting the boy on the head, Santa said, "Good boy."

As the old saying goes, "Them that gots is them that gets." But with God's grace it is the opposite: "Them that don't got is them that gets."

I have seen the film *The Sound of Music* more than just about any human being I know. I love it! Despite all of its schmaltz and sentimentality, I always find myself dabbing a tear from my eye at some point in the story. My favorite scene is when Maria learns, to her delight and dismay, that Captain Von Trapp loves her. They are standing gazing into each other's eyes under a gazebo, beside an alpine lake shimmering in the moonlight. She sings to him of the wonder that she, of all people, should be loved by someone as grand as he. She can't understand why one such as she should be so blessed. There has to be some explanation. Why her? She is sure she must have had a wicked and miserable childhood, but sometime, somewhere she must have done something good, for "nothing comes from nothing, nothing ever could."

In the world it is true that nothing comes from nothing, nothing ever could. But with God all things come from nothing! He created the universe out of nothing. He made the sun, the moon and the stars out of nothing. And he gives us his grace and love and promise out of "nothing"; for no other reason than that is just the way it is with him—he loves us, that's all.

Look at God's promise to Abram and Sarai through the eyes of Job's hard-earned humility. God, he discovered, owed him no explanations for what he was doing with him. Job could lay no demands on God. God is not in Job's, or in anyone else's, debt. He is absolutely and sovereignly free to do whatever he, in his wisdom and power and goodness, deems right. He consults with no one, least of all us.

The hard side of that freedom is what Job ran into. The tender side is what Abram and Sarai meet. The hard side makes us humble. The tender side makes us hopeful. But it's the humility that makes possible the hope. It's knowing that God owes us nothing that makes his gifts so sweet and his generosity so astonishing.

Active Waiting

Abram and Sarai don't know it, but they've got a long wait out ahead of them. It will be twenty-four long years before God gives them the son he has promised. It's one thing to have twenty-four years to wait when you're twenty years old; quite another when you're seventy-five, as Abram was. And it's going to be a very special kind of waiting. We usually think of waiting as a passive exercise, just biding time until we get the thing we're waiting for. Maybe we'll engage in some kind of diversion as we wait, but that's incidental to the waiting itself, which really isn't something we do. But biblical waiting, the kind of waiting Abram and Sarai did, and which you and I must learn to do, is a very active kind of waiting. It's a faith-journey, the waiting of a pilgrimage. We can only wait for God to give us what we cannot get ourselves; but, paradoxically, we must move toward it in faith as we wait, asking, seeking and knocking as Jesus commanded (Lk 11:9-10).

We are told that with God's gracious promise to Abram and Sarai there was also his command to get up and "go to the land that I will show you." Get up and go—that's the kind of waiting that was required of Abram. In the events that follow, we are told that Abram made three moves, and the episode ends with the statement: "Then Abram set out and continued toward the Negev" (Gen 12:1, 9). Abram becomes a man on the move, a traveler and a pilgrim. That's the nature of his waiting. Centuries later, when the Hebrews brought their offerings to the Tabernacle, they confessed their faith with reference to Abram, their creed beginning with the phrase, "My father was a *wandering* Aramean" (Deut 26:5, emphasis mine).

So with us. The apostle Paul wrote that "Those who believe are children of Abraham" (Gal 3:7). Believe what? God's promises, fulfilled and anticipated in Jesus Christ. To believe God's promises is to trust that he will keep them and to wait for them as Abram and Sarai did—en route! To wait is to journey in faith toward the things God has promised. Like all journeys, it has its past, present and future, and requires a definite attitude toward each of these time dimensions.

The past—God says, "Leave it." To wait for God's promise demanded that Abram turn his back on his idolatrous past in the land of his father. It meant that he exchange life in a flourishing civilization, with large, well-planned cities, established law codes and sophisticated arts and sciences, for life in the backward hill country of eastern Canaan. As good as any of the things that he once knew might be, to wait for God's promise meant saying no to his past and leaving it behind.

To wait on God, we must travel with Abram and Sarai, and Paul, who said of his wait, "I leave the past behind and with hands outstretched to whatever lies ahead I go straight for the goal— my reward the honour of my high calling by God in Christ Jesus."[2] To wait on God is to see our past, especially the sins and failures of our past, as merely footprints. It says, "This is where I was," never, "This is where I'm stuck."

The present—God says, "Go." Abram's present was to be lived in transit. In the account of Abram's call in Genesis 12, there is a great symbolic contrast between altars and tents. As he travels, Abram *builds* altars to God, but he *pitches* his tents. His dwelling was temporary; the only thing permanent in Abram's life was what he did as a testimony to the God whose promise he was waiting for. Nearly 900 years later, as he dedicated the monies for the building of the great temple, King David would pray to God, "We are aliens and strangers in your sight, as were all our forefathers" (1 Chron 29:15, emphasis mine). Faithful to his call to wait for God's promise, King David continued to live as his father Abram. To wait on God is to see our present, also, as a footprint. It says "This is where I am now," never "This is where I must stay."

To wait for God in the active wait of the faith-journey is like swinging on a trapeze. If you are like me, and afraid of heights, you feel you are doing something extraordinarily daring just to be up there. But the object of swinging on a trapeze is to swing just long enough to let go! You stay on the trapeze just long enough to gain the momentum necessary to let go of the trapeze you're on to grab hold of the next swinging trapeze. To lay hold of God's promise and God's future, we must let go of the past and the present and whatever else we have been holding on to and experience what has been called the "creative insecurity" of moving on to the next stage, the next season in our journey.

The Music of the Future

The future—God says, "I will show you." The future is the dimension of waiting and the dominant tense for Abram and Sarai. For them to receive God's promise, they had to exchange the known, their past and present, for the unknown, God's future. The author of the book of Hebrews, in the New Testament, provides a masterful commentary on the saga of Abram and Sarai and their waiting faith when he writes,

> Now faith is being sure of what we hope for and certain of what we do not see. . . . By faith Abraham, when called to go to a place he would later receive as his inheritance, obeyed and went, even though he did not know where he was going. By faith he made his home in the promised land like a stranger in a foreign country; he lived in tents, as did Isaac and Jacob, who were heirs with him of the same promise. For he was looking forward to the city with foundations, whose architect and builder is God. (Heb 11:1, 8-10)

There we see again the paradox of the future orientation of biblical waiting: Abram must wait, therefore he must go—to a future that only God can give him. He must go he knows not where. This is the tension that animates the life of faith.

It's not uncommon to see people today going about their daily activities wearing headphones plugged into a radio or tape player. It irritates me to try to carry on a conversation with such people. As we talk, I get the feeling that whatever is going on inside the headphones is the reality, and I am but a shadow. From personal experience I know how powerful and compelling the music can be, and how distant and uninteresting everything else seems while the music is being injected, as it were, right into one's skull. The presence of that device over my head and ears sets me apart.

As negative as it may be for human contact, let the headphones be a picture of what the wait and the walk of faith is about. To hear God's promise and call is to hear something that perhaps no one else around us can hear. It is to feel ourselves begin to tap our toes and move gently to the beat of the music, perhaps to the bewilderment of those watching us. The music we hear is the music of God's future. Hope is hearing the tune; faith is to dance to it now.[3] It's not that we live our lives in the future, it's that the future begins to live right now, in our present!

In our waiting, God calls us out of ourselves to make us new people. Poet Luci Shaw captures the spirit of this when she writes, as though God is beckoning to us,

leap out from your reedy shallows.
Dive into the moving water.
Eyeless, learn to see truly.
Find in my folly your true sanity.[4]

Worth the Journey!

A great demand is laid upon us when we are called, as Abram and Sarai were, to leave our past and present and travel to God's future, waiting for his promise. But God's great demand, his "you must," is completely overshadowed by his "I wills." "I will make you a great nation . . . I will bless you . . . I will make your name great . . . I will bless those who bless you . . . and all peoples will be blessed through you" (Gen 12:1-3). They are heaped up, one upon another, into a mountain of grace and mercy. Our faltering steps forward seem so big to us, but they are minuscule compared to the steps God has already taken and will take.

When my first son was but four years old, my wife and I took him to Disneyland for the first time. When I enter the gates of the Magic Kingdom, something magic happens to me—I regress emotionally, about thirty years. When we arrived, the first thing I wanted to do, as I rushed through the park, practically dragging my son by the hand, was to get in line for my favorite ride—Space Mountain, a roller coaster of a ride with a spaceship motif and lots of speed and wild turns. This was to be Danny's first exposure to an amusement park ride.

The Disney people must have a rationale for the way they organize the long lines for their rides—a "queuing theory" for the wait. I think they must set it up so you can hear, as you wait, the screams of those already on the ride. Listening to all that, by the time you get to the ride you are so agitated yourself that the ride takes on even greater, more terrifying psychological proportions. As we got closer, it finally began to dawn on me that this ride might not be the best introduction of my son to the wonders of amusement parks. Remembering how sensitive his stomach can be, I began to mentally calculate how long it had been since he had eaten breakfast. I asked him, "Danny, are you sure you want to ride this thing?" (As though it had been his idea, not mine!) He looked up at me with trusting eyes and said, "Yes, Daddy."

Thus we got into our little spaceship, him completely at ease with his good father's judgment. Moments later, as the spaceship twisted and lurched madly over the track at high speed, the knuckles on his chubby little hands grew white as they gripped the bar across our lap, and his little body became one with mine. In a desperate effort to reassure him and calm his stomach, I began to shout frantically, "Isn't this fun! Isn't this fun!" When the ride was over, and we walked shakily back to his concerned mother, I asked him if he ever wanted to do it again. He said, "Not just now, Daddy."

The ride was wild and frightening, but—and here's the point of this little story—while we rode together, Danny stayed closer to me than he ever had, or has since. And he listened to my voice better than he ever does. The paradoxical journey of waiting, moving from the known to the unknown, the seen to the unseen of God's future, will have some terrifying moments in it. Ease and predictability are not among God's promises. But as we wait, as we journey, we will find ourselves clinging to God as never before, and listening for his voice as if our life depended on it! That, in itself, makes the waiting worth the while.

Notes

[1] A phrase of Helmut Thielicke's, used in his excellent little book *The Silence of God* (Grand Rapids, Mich.: Eerdmans, 1962). See pages 10-21.

[2] Philippians 3:14; J. B. Phillips's paraphrase, *The New Testament in Modern English* (New York: Macmillan, 1960).

[3] Rubem Alves, *Tomorrow's Child* (New York: Harper and Row, 1972), p. 195.

[4] Luci Shaw, "The Foolishness of God," from *A Widening Light,* ed. Luci Shaw (Wheaton, Ill.: Harold Shaw, 1984), p. 134.

A few scabs dappled his white skin where he had scraped the bald spot on top of his head. That's most of what I saw of him that day as he sat in my office. He kept his head down as he spoke, his eyes not willing to meet mine for more than a moment. I watched the way his knuckles bulged as he rubbed his hands together in anguish.

I had lost count of the number of times I had sat with him to hear his confession. It was more of the same this time—same old sins, same old failures. But it was different, too. He was about to give up on trying to be a Christian.

He wanted to know, "Won't I ever get to the place in my life where I won't have to ask God to forgive me for the things I do?"

Heaven knows I wanted to say, "Yes! You will!" But I couldn't. I knew that he—and I—will never outgrow our need for the mercy and forgiveness of God. Not until the resurrection, that is.

But that we have to wait for.

CHAPTER FIVE
A Mirror, Not a Model

—— GENESIS 12:10-20 ——

I read of a man who had never attended a church, but who decided, at the urging of a friend, to go one Sunday. A few minutes after the service began, he slipped nervously into the back pew of the sanctuary. Just as he did the congregation was praying a unison confession of sin: "We have done the things we ought not to have done, and have left undone the things we ought to have done." He breathed a sigh of relief and thought: "At last! I've finally found my kind of people!"

Abram is our kind of people. He's not so much a *model* of waiting on God as he is a *mirror*—a mirror of what we all know waiting is really like. He doesn't always match our ideal versions of how we should be as we wait.[1]

It's true, Abram was a hero when he first obeyed God's call to leave the security of his home and go to the place that God would show him. But he was hard to identify with then, wasn't he? His story sounded a bit like the testimonies we hear through the Christian media, telling of how drug addicts and Mafia chieftains came to faith in Christ and immediately left what they were doing to follow him. The stories are stirring, but remote. Most of us live out our lives in much more pedestrian circumstances, from nine to five amid deadlines and diapers. From bitter experience, we are too aware of how the immediate and momentary can completely capture our attention to be convinced that Abram's adventure of faith can be our adventure too.

A Famine in the Promised Land

But now we have a mirror—and Abram becomes someone we can identify with. After Abram gets to the promised land, we read the ominous line, "Now there was a famine in the land" (Gen 12:10). A famine—in the promised land! Isn't that a contradiction in terms? Promised lands aren't supposed to have famines, are they?! But sometimes they do. Sometimes the very place God brings us to is the place where we know the greatest hunger. What we do with our hunger as we wait is crucial.

Abram doesn't do very well with his. When he gets to the promised land, not only does he run into a famine, but he finds it already occupied by a hostile people who will take a dim view of his conviction that it will one day be his. He's like the man who has just watched escrow close on his dream house only to discover, to his horror, that the structure has termites and his neighbors are drug dealers. What's a man to do but pack up and get out? Maybe he heard God wrong, or worse, God got it wrong. So he leaves the promised land and heads south for Egypt, where for centuries the Nile River had insulated the land from famine.

But once in Egypt, Abram is faced with another crisis. His beautiful wife, Sarai, is too good-looking for the ruthless Pharaoh to resist—not that the Pharaoh ever worried about resisting anything; he was the ruler of the most powerful and ancient civilization of that day. When Abram arrived in Egypt, sometime around 1900 B.C., he looked at pyramids that were already 700 years old. Pharaoh didn't have to explain to anyone what he did; he just did it. With him it was like the question "What do you call a man who is 6 feet 8 inches, weighs 285 pounds and has 19-inch arms?" The answer: "You call him 'Sir.' " Abram is without any resources or leverage of any kind. All he has is a promise from God that will impress the Pharaoh no more than it would have the inhabitants of the promised land in Canaan. What can he do? He knows Pharaoh will want Sarai for his harem. And he knows the king will not hesitate to arrange for some sudden calamity to overtake Abram, leaving Sarai a poor widow that Pharaoh will magnanimously take into his household to protect and care for.

Abram ponders what to do and decides there is only one thing he can do: He will tell everyone that Sarai is his sister, and that way Pharaoh can have what he wants—Sarai—and Abram can have what he wants—his hide. Of all the unrecorded conversations in the Bible, I would have loved to have heard this one! Picture Abram sitting down with his beloved Sarai, the one he promised to love and cherish till death them did part, saying, "Say you are my sister, so that I will be treated well for your sake and my life will be spared because of you" (Gen 12:13).

As anyone could have predicted, Pharaoh saw Sarai, wanted Sarai, and married Sarai. As was the custom of the day, he paid her "brother" a rich dowry of sheep, cattle, donkeys, camels and servants. As Abram sits in his tent, checking his newly enlarged bank account, we see this great man of faith in quite a different light, don't we? We find him to be a lot more like us than we might have thought before; he is a man who has to get on, who has to live in the "real world," who acts prudentially and accepts the limitations of the circumstances in which he finds himself. After all, it's not his fault that there's a famine in the so-called promised land and that Pharaoh is such an arrogant and rapacious man. That is just the way the world is, and he has to live in it. Who can blame him—or us—if we shave a little off here, smooth things a bit there, make a few calculations and take care of business? There are limits to just how long a man or woman can wait, aren't there?

The honeymoon for Pharaoh and Sarai is over before it has begun. The day she arrives at the palace, God afflicts him and his household with certain unspecified diseases. Pharaoh is no epidemiologist, but he doesn't miss the correlation between Sarai's arrival and the sickness. So he sends for the brother of this lovely bride who appears to have brought along with her the palace plague. Abram comes and, under interrogation, breaks down and admits the deception. Pharaoh is enraged and indignant, and what follows is one of the most humiliating events in Abram's life. This pagan king, this idolater, this arrogant despot, lectures Abram, the man of God, on ethics! "What have you done to me? . . . Why didn't you tell me she was your wife? Why did you say, 'She is my sister,' so that I took her to be my wife?" (Gen 12:18-19).

This story does give us all something to identify with, doesn't it? We often act out of fear and selfish desires. If we were making a film epic of Abram's life, we are no longer sure how we would cast him. Based on the first nine verses of Genesis, chapter twelve, it would have been Charlton Heston. But now, who would it be? Pee Wee Herman, I think.

The Bright Side of Failure

And what do you see in the mirror? The brilliance of a Charlton Heston, or the sometimes-foolish failures of a Pee Wee Herman? When we look at Abram we see a person who, like us, struggles with waiting, and who sometimes fails pathetically. It was a great triumph of faith for Abram to leave his home for a land that God would show him. It was a wretched failure for Abram to go down to Egypt in fear and attempt his tawdry little deception of Pharaoh. But triumph and failure always go together in the wait of faith. They are the head and tail of the same coin. Show me a person who has had no struggle with waiting, whose faith has known no swings between victory and defeat, and I'll show you a person who has never really trusted God with his or her life.

To wait on God is to struggle and sometimes to fail. Sometimes the failures teach us more than the successes. For the failures teach us that to wait on God is not only to wait *for* his mercy, but to wait *by* his mercy. What is it you are waiting for? I don't have to know the specifics to know that my waiting and yours have this much in common—at bottom, we are both waiting for God to show us his kindness, his mercy. The glory hidden in our failures is the discovery that the very thing we wait for is what we wait by! The success of our waiting lies not in who we are, but in who God is. It is not our strength that will pull us through to the end, it is God's amazing grace and mercy:

Through many dangers, toils and snares,

I have already come;

'Twas grace hath brought me safe thus far,
And grace will lead me home.[2]

God's mercy is the home we wait for and what will get us there. Mercy is the goal of the wait, and its means!

Take note: God does not reject Abram for what he does in Egypt. Despite Abram's shameless behavior, the man actually leaves Egypt richer than when he arrived. When God first called Abram and made his promise to him, it was made without regard to his moral goodness. When Abram went down to Egypt and pulled his sordid shenanigan, the promise continued despite his moral lapse. That tells us God starts with us where we are, in order to take us to the place we need to be. In Christ, he took on human flesh and became as we are so that, in the words of the church father Irenaeus, we might become as he is. That is the outrage of his grace and mercy. That is why Jesus told the good religious folk of his day that the tax collectors and prostitutes were entering the kingdom of God ahead of them. Unlike the "good" people who thought their moral goodness set them in a right relationship to God, these "bad" people knew their moral bankruptcy and were willing to simply cast themselves on God's mercy.

That is all that matters to God. That is what faith is—beginning the journey. It is never as important to God where you are on the journey, as it is that you are indeed on the journey. Where you are going is what matters to God, not where you happen to be at the moment. You may start with God no matter what mess your life may be in at the present time.

In Ten Words or Less . . .
In his autobiography, *Brother to a Dragonfly,* Will Campbell re-

calls his friendship with a profane and brilliant skeptic named
P. D. East. He and East had often argued to a standstill about the
truth of Christianity. One day, as they rode together in a car, East
came at him from a surprising angle.

> Just tell me what this Jesus cat is all about. I'm not too bright
> but maybe I can get the hang of it. . . . If you could tell me
> what the hell the Christian faith is about maybe I wouldn't
> make an ass out of myself when I'm talking about it. Keep it
> simple. In ten words or less, what's the Christian message? . . .
> Let me have it. Ten words.

Campbell thought hard for several minutes. What would be your
answer, in ten words or less? Campbell's was this: "We're all
bastards but God loves us anyway."

East swung his car over onto the shoulder of the road and
stopped. He asked Campbell to repeat his definition. He obliged.
East counted the number of words on his fingers. "I gave you a
ten word limit. If you want to try again you have two words left." [3]

The language in that definition is raw, but is it really any different from the words of the Bible which say, "Christ died for our
sins"? We have anaesthetized ourselves to the word *sin*. It no
longer stabs us with grief and the fear of a holy God. To say that
we are sinners is to say that we are all the misbegotten enemies
of God, bastards every one, deserving judgment and death.

It is only as we see the enormity of our sin that we can appreciate the magnitude of God's mercy to us. If Christ would die for
sinners, if he would love us misbegotten ones enough to do that
before we even cared for him (and whether or not we ever did),
then how much more, now that we have believed in him, will
he preserve us by that same love? If we can believe the first word
of the gospel, that Christ died for us, it should be no problem

whatsoever to believe the next word of the gospel, that he will preserve us after we believe even when we fail. We are saved by God's mercy and we wait by God's mercy. Faith is not our ability to hold on to God, but simply trusting in his ability to hold on to us.

Abram's story is a story of suspense and profound tension. Will God keep his promise? Can he, in the face of Abram's failures? He can and he will! But will Abram trust God and wait on him? Is he able? Probably not! But against all odds God will keep his promise, and Abram will somehow manage to believe, in spite of himself. The entire saga of this man seems to be one narrow escape after another, with God providing the thrills and the hope. Karl Barth was right when he termed God's grace his great "nevertheless."

And so it is with us. The apostle Paul calls Abram the father of faith. How well did our daddy do with waiting? Like his children have done ever since, like you and I do—not always very well! Will God keep his promise to us? He will. Will we believe him? Probably not, a good deal of the time. But God will emerge the victor in our struggle to listen to him and trust him.

To wait is to struggle and sometimes to fail. We all know too well that the slightest whisper of temptation can be heard more clearly than the loudest call to duty. It is the experience of us all that a good scare teaches us better than good advice. Knowing that about ourselves, we need to tell and retell the great story of God's merciful triumph over Abram, for his triumph over him is to be over each of us as well.

What freedom is there for us waiters in believing that! Robert Schuller asks, "What great thing would you attempt if you knew you could not fail?" The question is designed to break us out of our mental ruts and to think of the possibilities of our lives. I would change it slightly and ask, "What great thing would you wait for if you knew God would not fail you—if you knew that even your sins and failures would not destroy God's faithfulness to you?" The answer to that question can fill us with hope and tenacity in waiting.

A Bad Piece of Meat

Peter once asked Jesus how many times he should forgive one who has sinned against him. Suggesting a possible statute of limitations, he asked, "Up to seven times?" Jesus answered, "I tell you, not seven times, but seventy-seven times" (Mt 18:21-22). Jesus was not expanding the outside limits of forgiveness, he was exploding them! He was saying we should always forgive, times without number. At first that is bad news, of a sort. It tells me I must keep on forgiving the nuisance who repeatedly offends me. But underneath it is unimaginably good news—it tells me that is how often God forgives me! He simply doesn't give up on me. His promises will not fail because of my failures.

Søren Kierkegaard prayed a lovely prayer that I often pray as my own when I doubt this: "Father in heaven! Hold not our sins up against us but hold us up against our sins, so that the thought of thee, when it wakens, should not remind us of what we have committed but of what thou didst forgive, not of how we went astray but of how thou didst save us!"[4] As we trust a God as merciful and as faithful as this—who will not hold our sins against us, but who will hold us up against our sins—even the memory of our sins can become a cause for joy. We can be filled with hope as we wait for God's promise because we know our sins will not cancel his promise.

Where I live in Southern California, the air of summer evenings is usually filled with the delicious smells of meat barbecuing over charcoals. Fine meat cooked over a fire is a treat in my household. If the meat is a prime cut of tender beef, there is not much I can do to make it better. It needs only to be slapped on the charcoal broiler and left to cook. But if the meat is tough, there is a lot I have to do to make it good. The best way I know is to let it soak in a rich marinade of wine and fine spices, the longer the better. When all of these good things soak into the fiber of the bad beef, it gradually takes on their characteristics and becomes tender and delicious.

Please pardon the comparison, but when God got us, he got a lousy cut of beef! We're tough with the gristle of unbelief and stubbornness. And we won't be good until we've been marinaded for a lifetime—waiting and soaking in the rich juices of his relentless love and patience. We need not worry about how well we will do. We need only trust how well God does. As Paul said, "I know whom I have believed, and am convinced that he is able to guard what I have entrusted to him for that day" (2 Tim 1:12b).

Notes

[1]"A mirror, not a model," is a pregnant phrase used by William Sanford LaSor, David Allan Hubbard, and Frederick William Bush, *Old Testament Survey* (Grand Rapids, Mich.: Eerdmans), 1982.

[2]From the hymn "Amazing Grace."

[3]Will Campbell, *Brother to a Dragonfly* (New York: Seabury, 1979), p. 220.

[4]Perry D. LeFevre, ed., *The Prayers of Kierkegaard* (Chicago, Ill.: University of Chicago Press, 1956), p. 21.

I stared down into the dregs of the cup of coffee. *What he was saying made no sense at all.* Not only was it ridiculous for us to consider tithing our meager income, but what did that have to do with what we were there for?

My wife and I began our life together with me unemployed—I was fired from my job two months before we were married. The only work I could find was selling swimming pools for a company owned by a friend of mine. In six months, I sold exactly two pools. We didn't have enough money to both pay the rent and buy the food, much less to keep up the insurance on the car. Life was boiled down to the bare essentials—food, clothing and shelter. We could pick one.

Now here we were, sitting in the kitchen of the man who bought the second pool I sold, waiting for him to write a check, and listening to him deliver a discourse on tithing. He said it was a practical way of living out Matthew 6:33, of seeking first the kingdom of God, of putting God first—and letting him take care of everything else we might need. It was crazy, but I was impressed by what he said. In fact, I was overwhelmed.

On the way out to the car this man, who knew nothing of our financial straits, said to my wife and me, "I hope you don't think I'm nuts, but as I was praying this morning I felt God wanted me to talk to you about tithing." I mumbled something noncommittal, like a thank-you for sharing his ideas with us, and drove away.

I asked Lauretta what she thought of what he said and discovered that she had the same experience I had. I can still remember the spot on the road we were on when we decided to tithe. It was wonderful! No sense of "ought," just the exhilaration of embarking on a great adventure. We were failing miserably at taking care of ourselves. Why not see if God could do better? It was scary, but what the heck! Could we possibly get any poorer?

Would it work? We would have to wait and see. (It did!)

CHAPTER SIX
The Road Less Traveled

—— GENESIS 13:1-18 ——

There is a saying: "When a man with experience meets a man with money and no experience, it is the man with the experience who gets the money, and the man with the money who gets the experience." As we read more of the story of Abram's waiting, his nephew Lot appears to be the man with all the experience and Abram appears to be the man with all the money. At first glance it seems that Lot walks away with all of the money and all Abram walks away with is a very bitter experience.

Abram and Lot, who has been traveling with Abram, are grazing their flocks in a land that is short on good pasture. Their hired men begin to fight with one another over grazing space and water. So Abram the elder, the uncle, goes to Lot the younger, the nephew, and says, "Let's not have any quarreling between you and me, or between your herdsmen and mine, for we are brothers. Is not the whole land before you? Let's part company. If you go to the left, I'll go to the right; if you go to the right, I'll go to the left" (Gen 13:8-9).

What does Lot do when he is made this very generous offer by Abram? He takes every advantage of Abram he can, that's what he does. "Lot looked up and saw that the whole plain of the Jordan was well watered, like the garden of the LORD, like the land of Egypt, toward Zoar. (This was before the LORD destroyed Sodom and Gomorrah.) So Lot chose for himself the whole plain of the Jordan and set out toward the east. The two men parted company: Abram lived in the land of Canaan, while Lot lived among the cities of the plain and pitched his tents near Sodom" (Gen 13:10-12). Lot and his herds move to the fertile and well-watered Jordan plain, and Abram moves back into the rocky and arid hill country. Lot pitches his tents near the economic and cultural centers of Sodom and Gomorrah; Abram looks for a place to live among the hostile mountain tribes of Canaan.

No to Self

What makes this so puzzling is the story immediately preceding it, in which Abram plays the opposite role. There he is the one with the experience and Pharaoh is the one with the money. But it is a chastened Abram we meet in this story, a wiser Abram, a man who has learned a vital lesson about waiting. To borrow from the title of Scott Peck's excellent best seller and from Robert Frost's poem, he is now learning that if he is going to take the journey of faith and wait on God, it will mean traveling down a road that few take. He is learning that if waiting on God means trusting God's promise, then it means no longer trusting himself, for to say yes to God is to say no to self.

92

How do we know this about Abram? By his response to the next crisis in his life. Instead of taking matters into his own hands, as in Egypt, and using his own available wits and resources, he leaves it all to God. That, in a word, is what it means for him to no longer trust himself. There is not enough land to feed Abram and his family and Lot and his family. He could pull rank on Lot and flex his muscles and get a better deal, but instead he tells him to take what he wants and he will take what is left. His future well-being is in God's hands, not his own, so he will settle down and wait to see what God will do.

A family was awakened by the piercing blare of their smoke detector to discover that their house was on fire. The father ran into the kids' room and carried the eighteen-month old baby out in his arms, dragging his four-year-old in tow by the hand. They were halfway down the stairs when the little boy realized that he had left his teddy bear in his room. He broke away from his father to run back to get it. In the furor and confusion, Dad didn't notice that his son wasn't with him until he got outside. By now the boy was trapped by the fire and smoke in his second-floor bedroom. Smoke swirled around him as he coughed and cried out the window, "Daddy! Daddy! Help me!"

His dad yelled from below, "Jump out the window, Andy! I'll catch you!"

"But I can't see you, Daddy!"

Daddy shouted back, "That's O.K., son, I can see you! Jump!"

Abram can't see *what* is out there, but he knows *who* is out there, so like the little boy, he can jump. He doesn't have to worry about what will happen if Lot gets the good land and he doesn't, because he knows his future well-being is in God's hands, not his own. That's why Abram can be so generous, magnanimous and loving. He knows he doesn't have to fight for himself, and that sets him free to love.

That is the dynamic of waiting faith: it expresses itself in love. There is a version of pop psychology that says we cannot love others until first we are able to love ourselves. There is an element of truth in that dictum, but it doesn't go deep enough. The Bible says we are not able to love, truly love, until we feel secure enough to take the risk of looking out for others instead of ourselves. When Scripture says we love because God first loved us (1 Jn 4:19), it is underlining that truth. It is saying that trust in God's love and care for us is more basic to our emotional well-being and ability to love others than even a healthy self-esteem. When I really believe that I am secure in the loving arms of my heavenly Father, then I am finally free to stop worrying about how *I* am doing and can start being concerned about how *you* are doing. This is where faith and ethics connect.

Trekking with a companion through a high pass in the Himalayas, the great Indian Christian Sadhu Sundar Singh came upon the figure of a nearly frozen man, lying unconscious in the snow. Singh began immediately to try to revive him. But his traveling companion protested: "We shall lose our lives if we burden ourselves with him." But Singh insisted that they stay and help the man. Dismayed at the futility of the effort, his companion abandoned him. Singh somehow managed to get the body of the man up on his shoulders and continued to walk, carrying him. The physical exertion warmed him and the stricken man, and eventually revived him. Soon the two men were walking side by side. Two days later they came upon the frozen body of Singh's original companion, who had chosen to travel alone. Singh said the experience was a living illustration of what Jesus meant when he said, "Whoever wants to save his life will lose it, but whoever loses his life for me and for the gospel will save it" (Mk 8:35).[1]

Our Lord taught that we will all lose our lives, our selves, by death. We have no choice in the matter; one day each of us must let go. The choice is not *whether,* but *when.* The difference between a Christian and an unbeliever is essentially here—the Christian chooses to die to self now, by surrendering the sovereignty of self to the sovereignty of God. The Christian lets go of what he or she has now for the sake of something that God will give in the future. It's a sensible gamble for, as Jim Elliot put it, "He is no fool who will give up what he cannot keep to gain what he cannot lose." But everything in us resists that kind of proposition. It is the nature of a self to live by what it can see and control, not by what it cannot see or control. It is the nature of the self to hold on to things it can touch, rather than to hope in something it must wait for. To wait on God is to say no to that self.

Singh journeyed on a road less traveled, as did Abram. It is traveled by so few because so few are willing to stop trusting themselves as masters of their lives and instead start trusting God and waiting for his promises. That road is not only the road of faith, it is also the road to love—the free, unconditional, magnanimous love of God himself.

No to the World
The second thing Abram learned about waiting on this road less traveled is that faith is not only a no to self, but also a no to the world. When Abram and his nephew Lot parted company that day, it appeared that Lot had the better deal. When Lot chose the fertile, well-watered Jordan plain, Abram was forced back into the

hill country of Canaan where grazing was scarce, the culture was backward and the people were hostile. There was just one drawback for Lot—the people living there "were wicked and were sinning greatly against the LORD" (Gen 13:13). The cities of the plain, of which Sodom and Gomorrah were the worst, were so wicked that their names became synonymous with sin throughout the rest of the Bible. Two thousand years later, in the book of Revelation, at the very end of the Bible, the apostle John's vision of the city which is the embodiment of evil, the bastion of sin, is called "Sodom." That is what Lot is choosing along with good pastures. That is the way it always is with the world—what looks good on the outside may be rotten underneath.

Here we need to be careful to define what the Bible does and does not mean by "the world." It does not mean the created order—mountains, lakes, forests, deserts, seas, animals and people—especially people. The world, in this sense, is good, and we are to love it. What the Bible does mean by "the world" is all the sinful human systems and desires and values that align themselves against God as his competitor. The world, in this sense, is evil and rotten to the core. We are to hate this world. The lines could not be drawn any more sharply in the Bible.

John the apostle warns us: "Do not love the world or anything in the world. If anyone loves the world, the love of the Father is not in him. For everything in the world—the cravings of sinful man, the lust of his eyes and the boasting of what he has and does—comes not from the Father but from the world. The world and its desires pass away, but the man who does the will of God lives forever" (1 Jn 2:15-17).

Note that the Scripture says the world will pass away. It is transient and empty and fading. Therefore it has to sell itself and work hard to keep up its image. Its pitch is "trust me for security and power." Its image is life and health and fulfillment. It says, "You only go around once in life, so grab for all the gusto you can get." It says the pie is only so big, and there are more people who want pieces of it than there are pieces to be had. It says in that kind of world it is only the clever and the strong and the ruthless who survive.

As Abram and Lot stand together in the hills overlooking the Jordan plain with its fertile pastures and wicked cities, Lot buys the world's sales pitch—hook, line and sinker. It is not that it is wrong for him to want good pastures for his flocks and security for his family. It is not wrong that you and I want the equivalent of these things for ourselves. What is wrong is that he thinks as a man of the world, as we so often do, in calculating how these things are to be had.

For example, do you think that it is your responsibility to provide the necessities of life for yourself and, if you have one, for your family? Things like food and clothing and shelter? Right? Wrong! Jesus said those things are the responsibility of our heavenly Father. He said God holds us responsible for but one thing in life, to "seek first his kingdom and his righteousness . . ." (see also Mt 6:25-34). We are not to worry about things like food, clothing, shelter and how we are going to provide them. Our Father in heaven knows what we need. True, we are to work hard at the opportunities God gives us to make a living. And the New Testament has harsh words for those who refuse to work and to feed their families (1 Tim 5:8). But even the work we do to provide for ourselves and our families is a gift from our Father. Our great responsibility is to seek his kingdom and its righteousness, first and last. Everything else is up to God. If we think otherwise, we think as worldly wise sophisticates.

Abram is beginning to learn that the necessities of life are to be had by trusting God's promise. Lot still thinks they are to be had by trusting his own wits. Abram is learning that God's resources are unlimited and that he can trust God to provide for him in abundance out of his abundant resources. Lot still thinks there is just so much to go around and that he had better get his before someone else does, and if it means pitching his tent near Sodom, then that's just the way things are in the "real world." Beware of people who want to tell you about the so-called real world!

In 1924, Dallas Theological Seminary almost went bankrupt. On the day it was to foreclose at noon, Dr. Harry Ironside, the president, held a prayer meeting in his office. That day he prayed a prayer he had often prayed: "Lord, we know the cattle on a thousand hills are thine. Please sell some of them and give us the money." As he prayed with some staff and faculty, a tall Texas oilman walked into the receptionist's office and told the secretary: "I just sold two carloads of cattle in Fort Worth. I've been trying to make a business deal go through and it won't work, and I've been compelled to give this money to the seminary. I don't know if you need this, but here's the check." The secretary burst into the room where the men were praying and said to Dr. Ironside, "Harry, God just sold the cattle!"[2]

God Room

Abram knows God can sell the cattle whenever he chooses, so he walks by faith, not by sight. Lot walks by sight, not by faith. There is no "God room" in his vision. "God room" was a favorite term of Bob Pierce, the irrepressible founder of World Vision. By

"God room," he meant the gap between what was humanly achievable and what could happen only if God intervened. It was Pierce's conviction that life should be lived with lots of "God room." That he did. And though he drove people crazy with what so often seemed to be his fiscal irresponsibility, he was used of God in a mighty way to launch one of the greatest Christian outreaches of this century. He refused to let the so-called real world dictate to him what he would do for God. He lived life trusting and waiting for God to keep his promises.[3]

Our experience of God Room may not be as spectacular as a Harry Ironside's or a Bob Pierce's. But it will be no less real. The opportunity to experience it will come every time we put God first in our lives—at work, with our finances, in our marriages and moral choices—even if it seems unreasonable or crazy.

So Abram and Lot part company. As Lot starts down the hill into the fertile Jordan valley and the cities of Sodom and Gomorrah, he travels a broad highway, a road that many choose. He will take his life and destiny into his own hands. He will choose comfort and ease that he can see over the promise of God that he cannot see. Later he will pay dearly for that choice. Jesus said many are called but few are chosen; broad is the way that leads to destruction and narrow the way that leads to life (Mt 7:13-14). The walk and the wait of faith are not the middle way between two extremes, but the narrow way between two precipices.

As Abram starts up the hill into the highlands of eastern Canaan and its backward culture and hostile people, he journeys on a road less traveled. He says yes to God's promise and no to himself and the world and settles down to wait. Abram will not regret the no to himself and to the world, for in the final analysis the no to himself is for the sake of himself, and the no to the world is for the sake of the world. Abram will get back everything he let go of—in greater abundance than he could have ever even dreamed of on his own. Even as Lot could still be seen from afar, moving down into Sodom, God said to Abram: "Lift up your eyes from where you are and look north and south, east and west. All the land that you see I will give to you and your offspring forever. I will make your offspring like the dust of the earth, so that if anyone could count the dust, then your offspring could be counted" (Gen 13:14b-17). It will all one day be his, but he will have to wait for it! It will take a while, but God will keep his promise. For now, all Abram needs to know is that God can be trusted and that he will keep his word—that it will be worth his while to wait.

In the summer of 1988, three friends and I climbed Mt. Lyell, the highest peak in Yosemite National Park. Two of us were experienced mountaineers; two of us were not. I was not one of the experienced two. Our base camp was less than 2,000 feet from the peak, but the climb to the top and back was to take the better part of a day due, in large part, to the difficulty of the glacier one must cross to get to the top. The morning of the climb we started out chattering and cracking jokes. As the hours past, and we trudged up the glacier, the two mountaineers opened up a wide gap between me and my less-experienced companion. Being competitive by nature, I began to look for shortcuts I might be able to take to beat them to the top. I thought I saw one to the right of an outcropping of rock—so up I went, deaf to the protests of my companion.

Perhaps it was the effect of the high altitude, but the significance of the fact that the two experienced climbers had not chosen this path did not register in my consciousness. It should have, for thirty minutes later I was trapped in a cul-de-sac of rock atop the Lyell Glacier, looking down several hundred feet of a sheer slope of ice, pitched at about a forty-five degree angle. It is one thing to climb up a glacier, and quite another to climb down or traverse it. I was only about ten feet from the safety of a rock, but one little slip and I wouldn't stop sliding until I landed in the valley floor some fifty miles away! It was nearly noon, and the warm sun had the glacier glistening with slippery ice. I was stuck and I was scared.

It took an hour for my experienced climbing friends to find me. Standing on the rock I wanted to reach, one of them leaned out and used an ice axe to chip two little footsteps in the glacier. Then he gave me the following instructions: "Ben, you must step out from where you are and put your foot where the first foothold is. When your foot touches it, without a moment's hesitation swing your other foot across and land it on the next step. When you do that, reach out and I will take your hand and pull you to safety." That sounded real good to me. It was the next thing he said that made me more frightened than ever. He continued, "But listen carefully: As you step across, do not lean into the mountain! If anything, lean out a bit. Otherwise, your feet may fly out from under you and you will start sliding down."

I don't like precipices. When I am on the edge of a cliff, my instincts are to lie down and hug the mountain, to become one with it, not to lean away from it! But that was what my good friend was telling me to do as I stood trembling on that glacier. I looked at him real hard. I searched my memory for anything I might have done to him in the past for him to harbor any ill will toward me. Was there any reason, any reason at all, that I should not trust him? I certainly hoped not! So for a moment, based solely on what I believed to be true about the good will and good sense of my friend, I decided to say no to what I felt, to stifle my impulse to cling to the security of the mountain, to lean out, step out, and traverse the ice to safety. It took less than two seconds to find out if my faith was well founded. It was.

To wait on God is to entrust your life to God in that way. The big difference is that the step of trust is a lifetime in the taking. It is a daily choice. That's what makes it so hard. My wife, Lauretta, once remarked to me, "I know I'd die for Christ. If I were put in front of a firing squad and commanded to renounce Christ or die, I know I'd say 'Shoot me!' That would be easy. The hard part is *living* for Christ, not dying for him." She is right. One huge, heroic act would be easier than a lifetime of little daily decisions, especially when it may take a lifetime to discover that the promises of God were worth the no we said to ourselves and to the world each day. But we have this to go on: They are spoken by one who is eminently deserving of our trust. We can safely stake everything on him!

Notes

[1]Quoted in *Parables, Etc.,* March 1983 (Saratoga, Calif.: Saratoga Press), p. 2.
[2]Quoted in *Parables, Etc.,* January 1984 (Saratoga, Calif.: Saratoga Press), p. 4.
[3]Franklin Graham with Jeanette Lockerbie, *This One Thing I Do* (Waco, Tex.: Word, 1983), p. 53.

I still *flush with embarrassment and shame when I* think about it. I had put on my best Carl Rogers counseling demeanor, asked lots of questions, listened sympathetically to all Tom said and fed it back to him. I did everything I could to understand his situation.

After about an hour and a half of this, as near as I could tell, Tom wanted to divorce his wife simply because he wasn't happy with her anymore. No cruelty was involved, no adultery—just boredom. Then I dropped Carl Rogers and tried to talk him out of it, to persuade him to recommit himself, to go the long haul with the woman he promised to love until death did them part. He listened to me for a while, and then said, "But Ben, what about happiness?" And here's the embarrassing part—I could think of nothing to say to him.

It had never occurred to me to tell him that he might have to wait to be happy.

CHAPTER SEVEN
Counterfeit
Faith

—— GENESIS 16:1-16 ——

One of the principal words in the Hebrew vocabulary of faith is a word that has found its way into our language. It is the word *amen.* To me, it suggests the picture of a man leaning on a staff to steady himself, or a tent pegged into solid ground. When Abram believed God he steadied himself on God's promise; he pegged his life into the solid ground of God's character; he trusted in the trustworthiness of God; he said "Amen!" to what God said. In the final analysis, that is all God asks of anyone.

It has been ten years since God promised a son to Abram and Sarai. It was hard to believe in then, when he was seventy-five years old, but he did, and the Scripture says that when he did, God credited Abram with righteousness for trusting him (Gen 15:6). Abram did well.

But what was difficult to trust at age seventy-five can be overwhelmingly so at eighty-five—especially if it concerns having a child. Add to this the fact that Abram's wife, Sarai, did not have the benefit of a direct revelation from God as Abram did, and you can see how the tension would begin to build between these two. Moreover, there was a creative option provided by their culture. If the wife was barren, she could, if she wished, give her husband one of her slave girls to impregnate and thus build a family.

Sarai wants a son and an heir just as much as Abram does. It's been so long since this alleged promise from God, and they're not getting any younger. Sarai is beginning to find it very difficult to believe Abram got the message from God straight. Here they are, ten years older and still no child. Maybe her dreamer of a husband exaggerated the Lord's claims a bit. Maybe all God wanted to do was to help those who help themselves. Maybe all God meant was for them to do what many other couples in their predicament would do.

Thus begins a story of counterfeit faith. We're going to learn that God doesn't help those who help themselves: he helps those who trust him.

> Now Sarai, Abram's wife, had borne him no children. But she had an Egyptian maidservant named Hagar; so she said to Abram, "The LORD has kept me from having children. Go, sleep with my maidservant; perhaps I can build a family through her." Abram agreed to what Sarai said. So after Abram had been living in Canaan ten years, Sarai his wife took her Egyptian maidservant Hagar and gave her to her husband to be his wife. He slept with Hagar, and she conceived. (Gen 16:1-4)

Sarai cannot stand the delay in God's promise. Neither can Abram. It isn't easy to wait. It demands persistence when common sense says "give up." It says "believe" when there is no present evidence to back it up. Faith is forged in delay. Character is forged in delay. The forge is the gap between the promise and the fulfillment. As gold is purified and shaped in the white-hot heat of a forge, so we and our faith are purified and shaped in waiting.

What we must get used to as we wait is that God's sense of time is radically different from ours. In Los Angeles, California, there is a fossil museum beside the La Brea tar pits. At the entrance of the museum is a painting of a ribbon, eighty-five feet long, representing five billion years of the earth's history. One inch equals five million years. Do you know how much space on that ribbon belongs to the history of the human race, from the cave men to the astronauts? Less than one-half inch! When I saw that ribbon, I just stared and wondered: What was God doing the other 84 feet 11½ inches? Why all those bizarre creatures we call dinosaurs, whose occupancy alone on this planet approached 100 million years? What was he doing with them? Only God knows.

One thing is certain—ten years cannot be much in his grand scheme. Nor a lifetime. Nor the two millennia since Christ ascended to his Father, promising to return one day. Part of what the forge does in the purification and shaping of our character is to help us begin to see time from God's perspective. It gives us God's view of things, and with it, the patience to wait. For, as Peter reminds us, "With the Lord a day is like a thousand years, and a thousand years are like a day" (2 Pet 3:8).

God's Little Helpers

But Abram and Sarai can't yet stand the delay. So they engage in a counterfeit faith. They become "God's little helpers." They decide to take up some of the slack God has apparently left in his plan. "Is it a son he wants us to have? Well, that can be arranged, no problem. There are ways. Abram, meet Hagar." That is counterfeit faith—getting God's work done for him using your own methods, not his. It is attempting to achieve Christian ends by non-Christian means.

At the beginning, such plans always look so well intentioned— and they often are—but in the end they always result in chaos. Watch what happens to the parties involved:

> When [Hagar] knew she was pregnant, she began to despise her mistress. Then Sarai said to Abram, "You are responsible for the wrong I am suffering. I put my servant in your arms, and now that she knows she is pregnant, she despises me. May the LORD judge between you and me." (Gen 16:4-5)

That is the kind of thing that always happens in counterfeit faith. When God is taken out of the center of our lives and our plans, our relationships with people also begin to break down. Hagar rubs her mistress's nose in her inadequacy. Whenever Sarai is within earshot, Hagar talks loudly and incessantly of the joys of pregnancy. When the two women's eyes meet, Hagar, the servant, no longer averts her gaze. Sarai is furious. In a rage, she goes to Abram and accuses him, inexplicably, of responsibility for the whole affair. Hagar's false pride and Sarai's false blame are matched only by Abram's false humility. He tells Sarai: "Your servant is in your hands. . . . Do with her whatever you think best." It's not hard to guess what Sarai will think best. "Then Sarai mistreated Hagar; so she fled from her" (Gen 16:6).

So much for their little plan to help God out. So much for all of our little plans. When God makes a promise, he means it, exactly as he says it. He doesn't want our help; he wants our trust.

To wait for God is to bow before his superior wisdom and timing when it comes to the things we want. It is to confess that he, not we, is the one in charge.

Who's in Charge?

In the spring of 1980 I spent six weeks flat on my back. My doctor had diagnosed me as suffering from a ruptured disc and had prescribed total rest. I was not to get up for anything, except to go to the bathroom. My first thought was, "At least I'll get a lot of reading done." Wrong! Lying flat on my back caused my eyes to misfocus, and all the reading I did was in one book, which took me the entire six weeks to get through. I was helpless.

I was also terrified. What was this all going to mean? How was I to take care of my family? What about the church? I was the only pastor it had, and I could do nothing for it. Out of sheer desperation I decided to pray for the church. I opened the church directory and prayed for each member of the congregation, daily. It took nearly two hours, but since there was nothing else I could do for the church, I figured I might as well pray for it. It was not piety that made me do it, it was boredom and frustration. But over the weeks the prayer times grew sweet. One day near the end of my convalescence, I was praying and I told the Lord, "You know, it's been wonderful, these prolonged times we've spent together. It's too bad I don't have time to do this when I'm well."

God's answer came swift and blunt. He said to me, "Ben, you have just as much time when you're well as when you're sick. It's the same twenty-four hours in either case. The trouble with you is that when you're well, you think you're in charge. When you're sick, you know you're not." That exchange changed my attitude toward prayer completely. Though I'm not the man of

109

prayer I should be, I'm not the man I was, either.

It's no accident that a biblical image for prayer is that of waiting on God. Because prayer is the exercise, par excellence, of those whose hope is in God, not themselves. Think of the two classical postures of prayer—kneeling, with hands folded, head bowed; or standing, with arms outstretched, hands open. Both speak of relinquishing our hold on things. Both are images of receptivity. Both say the work of our hands must give way to the work of God's hands. Psalm 123 is a great psalm of prayer and of hopeful waiting on God. In our prayers, as in all we do, we are to be like slaves whose eyes are fixed on the master—looking for his merest gesture or glance, a flick of the hand, an arched eyebrow, anything he would say to tell us what to do.

> I lift up my eyes to you,
>> to you whose throne is in heaven.
> As the eyes of slaves look to the hand of
>> their master,
>> as the eyes of a maid look to the
>> hand of her mistress,
> so our eyes look to the LORD our God,
>> till he shows us his mercy. (Ps 123:1-2)

Humility and hope are the essentials of waiting. But it is humility that makes hope possible. As the psalm suggests, we cannot wait and hope with grace until we are humble. Until you are clear that it is God, not you, who is the master and you, not God, who are the servant, you will feel your rights have been violated whenever you are forced to wait. You will resent your waitings and find every rationalization to take matters into your own hands. In other words, you cannot hope in God until you have ceased to hope in yourself.

This will be a hard and, in some ways, galling lesson for Abram and Sarai to learn. Abram seems to be right back where he was ten years ago in Egypt, doesn't he? Once again he is trying to second-guess God and take matters into his own hands. Hasn't he grown at all? Hasn't he learned anything?

Have you ever had that feeling about yourself? I have. There are times when I look at myself and I don't seem to be a bit different than I was at age thirteen. I still make the same old mistakes. I still have the same old flaws in my character. I still commit the same old sins. Spiritual growth is like moving upward in a spiral: as we move up, as we grow, we keep passing the same old places in our character. In one sense nothing changes; in another, everything changes, for as we grow we grow in the mercy of God, who forgives us and gives us mastery over sin. From the beginning of our walk with Christ right until the end, we never outgrow our need for his grace and forgiveness. That is the beauty of the Roman Catholic sacrament of extreme unction. The last rites administered to the dying are the words, "Lord have mercy!" It says that right up until we die, we are dependent on the mercy and grace of God.

The Waiting God

Herein lies the greatest mystery of our waitings. Through them all it is really God who is doing all the waiting! We think we are the ones waiting for him, but in reality it is he who waits for us. Earlier I quoted Peter's statement about God's sense of time (2 Pet 3:8). Peter wasn't reflecting on God's eternality when he said that. He was underscoring God's patience, his merciful waiting for us to come around to repentance. The rest of Peter's statement is: "The Lord is not slow in keeping his promise, as some under-

111

stand slowness. He is patient with you, not wanting anyone to perish, but everyone to come to repentance" (2 Pet 3:9). It makes no difference to God—a day or a thousand years, a thousand years or a day, it's all the same. However long it takes, he can wait until we open our eyes. If we wait it is because God is waiting for us to become the people he wants us to be. Our Lord's most famous picture of God's love is of a father standing in front of his house, his eyes fixed on the horizon, waiting for his foolish son to come home (Lk 15:11-24). Each of us, in his or her own way, is that son.

Part of the waiting God does for us is to see us through the consequences of our bad choices. Hagar is on her way back home to Egypt, and Abram and Sarai are glad to see her go. So is she. The whole affair has been a disaster, and everyone involved would just as soon let well enough alone. "She's gone," Abram and Sarai sigh in relief. "They're history," Hagar mutters to herself. But God intervenes.

> The angel of the LORD found Hagar near a spring in the desert; it was the spring that is beside the road to Shur. And he said, "Hagar, servant of Sarai, where have you come from, and where are you going?"
>
> "I'm running away from my mistress Sarai," she answered.
>
> Then the angel of the LORD told her, "Go back to your mistress and submit to her." The angel added, "I will so increase your descendants that they will be too numerous to count." (Gen 16:7-10)

God doesn't let things slide. Abram and Sarai would like to. Hagar would like to. But God will not. There has been a breach of trust and responsibility, and he will not sweep it under the rug. First the good news: Hagar receives a promise that is beyond her wildest dreams. She will be the mother of a great nation, and her descendants will be too numerous to count. Now the bad news: she is addressed by the angel as "Hagar, servant of Sarai," a title she definitely would like to get rid of! She must go back to her mistress, Sarai, and submit to her. God will not bypass what Abram and Sarai did to Hagar, nor will he let things slide with what Hagar has done to Abram and Sarai.

Tough Grace

That is the way it always is with the grace of God. He never simply looks the other way and lets things slip out the back door. Everything that has happened must be dealt with in some way. The choices we make, the things we do, all have consequences that must be faced. Abram and Sarai must look at the servant Hagar and her child every day for the next thirteen years. Hagar must go back and serve a woman who hates her guts. God's grace does not lift us out of our responsibilities. He doesn't give us a free ticket out of life's hardships. Rather, he sustains us in the midst of them all. As with God's promise to Abram and Sarai, so with Hagar: she must wait for it in the here and now of her life with all of its responsibilities, frustrations and injustices.

That usually runs counter to everything we want to do with God's grace and everything our world tells us to do with life's hardships. We are told we have a "right" to be happy and to eliminate the things that make for unhappiness. But God has a greater plan. A professor in a college ethics class presented his students with a problem. He said, "A man has syphilis and his wife has tuberculosis. They have had four children: one has died, the other three have what is considered to be a terminal illness. The mother is pregnant. What do you recommend?" After a spirited discussion, the majority of the class voted that she abort the child. "Fine," said the professor, "You've just killed Beethoven."[1] How many opportunities for courage and character have we aborted because we wanted out of a situation and were determined to get out—because we thought it was our God-given right to be happy? But happiness is not our right, but a gift.

The God Who Sees Us

And God is amazingly generous with the gift. Hagar goes back to serve her mistress, Sarai, and to bear the son of Abram. Before she leaves the spring where the angel of God met her, she gives God a name. Translated into English, it is, "You are the God who sees me" (Gen 16:13). For a slave girl who had no rights of her own, who was no more than a piece of property to her master, who was the victim of the arbitrary choice of another, there could be no better name for a God who had shown himself to her as a God of grace. He cared for her. He *saw* her. He saw *her!* To God, she was not a slave, she was Hagar! Certainly Abram and Sarai had not seen her. But she was a person, and she now knew that God saw her as such and that what happened to her mattered to him.

Her name for God calls to mind an encounter Jesus had with a Pharisee named Simon. He was at dinner at Simon's house when a woman, who was known in the town as a prostitute, walked into the dining room. Everyone stopped eating, as silence fell across the table. Eyes looked furtively about the room: Who did she know there? Of course, Simon was the prime suspect. The only sound to be heard was the sound of her bare feet padding across the stone floor. She knew Jesus! She stopped where he was reclining and knelt down, weeping. She let her tears fall on his very dirty feet, causing little rivulets of mud to run down their sides, as she wiped them with her hair. (Simon had omitted the common Middle Eastern courtesy of seeing to it that Jesus' feet were washed.) Then she broke open a vial of very expensive perfume and poured it on his feet, massaging it into his dry skin.

Simon was relieved and feeling self-righteous. He thought, "If this man were a prophet, he would know who is touching him." Presumably, if Jesus knew the kind of person who was touching him, he wouldn't let her. Then Jesus asked Simon a question. Beware when Jesus asks questions! They are rarely innocent. He asked, "Do you see this woman?" (Lk 7:36-50). The point was, Simon could not see that woman. To him, she was a category, a classification, a kind of woman—whore. She was not that to Jesus. She was a person, his sister, a daughter of God. Jesus has never seen a *kind* of person. He cannot; it is against his nature. He sees only you and me. To know that, to really be struck by that truth, is to be transformed. That is what happened to Hagar when she was turned around on the road to Egypt.

Old Puritan homes often had hanging on their walls an embroidered sampler with the words, "Thou God seest me." It was an adaptation of the name Hagar gave God, meant to serve as a warning to those who read it, something to sober them up as they pondered God's unblinking gaze, his unceasing watchfulness of them. It said, in effect, "He knows everything you think and do, so be very, very careful what you think and do!" Of course there is a truth in that sentiment, but that was not the intent of Hagar's name for God. It meant that God sees us as only a lover can see his beloved. He keeps his eyes on us because he wants to care for us, not because he wants to catch us in some sin. As the psalm says, "He who watches over Israel will neither slumber nor sleep. . . . The LORD will keep you from all harm—he will watch over your life" (Ps 121:4, 7).

"I have now seen the One who sees me," Hagar said as she left the spring. Then she gave the spring a name. She called it "Beer Lahai Roi" which means "well of the Living One who sees me" (16:13-14). Because she has seen the one who sees her, she is now free to go back to a very difficult situation at home and do the will of God there, even though it was not something she would have chosen for herself. She cannot know how things will turn out for her, but she knows she is seen by a God who sees what is ahead. Therefore she can go back to Sarai and her hatred and endure and have the child Ishmael. God's grace braces her for what lies ahead. It calls her to responsibility and courage in suffering. And that is what God's grace will do for you and me as we wait.

In Charles Colson's excellent book *Loving God,* he tells the remarkable story of a Russian Jew named Boris Nicholayevich Kornfeld. A doctor, Kornfeld found himself in the gulag for reasons that were never clear to him. His medical training made him an important person in the prison. He received no special privileges, but he was able to care for the sick. He did, however, have one odious task. It was to sign medical release forms for men who were to be punished in "the box." The box was just that— a tiny box a man would be forced to crouch in for days on end, in the Siberian winter, living in his own excrement, eating the meagerest of rations. The medical release certified that the victim was physically able to withstand the ordeal. The medical release was tantamount to a death warrant. Kornfeld intensely disliked doing this, but so did all the other doctors in the gulag. What could one do, anyway?

In the course of his duties, Kornfeld met a Christian, a nameless prisoner who told him of Jesus, his Messiah. What most captured Kornfeld's attention was the way this Messiah died. Like Kornfeld, he too had been arrested and imprisoned without just cause. Soon Kornfeld was converted. He had never known such joy! He was a prisoner on the outside, but he was free on the inside.

With his newfound faith, things began to change for Kornfeld, the first being that he would no longer sign the hated medical release forms. This infuriated the authorities, but they needed his medical expertise, so they let it slide. Now that Kornfeld was looking at the world through different eyes, other things had to change too. The prison had its "trustees," ruthless men who were prisoners themselves, but who served the prison authorities in exchange for certain privileges. These quislings would often wander the halls of the prison hospital, stuffing their mouths with the white bread set there on trays for men suffering from pellagra. White bread was all these men's stomachs could digest, and the trustees were taking it out of their mouths to stuff their own. Although it was officially illegal, no one ever said anything about it for fear of the trustees' revenge. But Kornfeld was a new man in Christ, and now he would speak!

One day he saw a trustee stealing the bread for the pellagra patients and he reported him to the authorities. The authorities could not have cared less, but to save face they were forced to punish the miscreant by putting him in the box for a few days. They were galled by what this nuisance Kornfeld had forced them to do, but took comfort in the fact that he would be murdered when the trustee got out of the box. Kornfeld was as good as dead. He knew it, and so did everyone else.

One of Kornfeld's patients was a young man recovering from

cancer surgery. Although heavily sedated with morphine, the patient recalled how Doctor Kornfeld would tell him of his faith in Christ as he drifted in and out of consciousness. As his condition improved, he grew more fascinated with what the doctor said. Then one day as Kornfeld left his room, he heard a commotion outside. It had happened; Kornfeld had been murdered, clubbed to death by eight mallet blows to the head.

End of story. A man became a Christian, but it didn't get him out of jail. He waited and waited and then he died there. That's all that happened. Well, not quite. On the strength of Kornfeld's witness, the cancer patient became a Christian. His name? Alexander Solzhenitsyn! With the possible exception of Mikhail Gorbachev, the most famous Russian in the world today is not a Communist, but a Christian!

Like Kornfeld, believing in Jesus will give us no short cuts in life. We will still have to face our gulags, whatever they may be. And like Kornfeld, we may die still waiting for what we wanted most deeply. We may die not knowing what God was up to as we waited. This side of eternity we will never know. But God will have been at work, fashioning a plan of such beauty and symmetry that our minds cannot now receive it.

Notes
[1]*His Magazine,* February 1984, inside back cover.

J immy *couldn't believe whose voice he heard on the* other end of the telephone line. How long had it been since they last spoke? Since the divorce was final, ten years ago? At least that long. He was shattered then, now merely cold and numb. He felt detached, floating somewhere above his head, as he listened to a conversation he never dreamed he'd have. What was she saying about having become a Christian last year?

Sheila was terrified. The words were coming in slurred spurts, between long, awkward pauses. Yes, it had been ten years—ten years that felt more like an abyss than a passage of time. When Sheila was near nervous collapse, a friend at work had told her about the new life in Jesus Christ. She had believed. And now she was talking to her former husband, long distance. His voice was flat amid the crackle of static. Would he, could he trust what she was going to say?

"I know this will be hard for you to believe, Jimmy, but I've become a Christian. I'm not calling to try to get back together. It's been too long. But I was thinking the other day about how much I must have hurt you when I left you ten years ago. Maybe I'm asking the impossible, but I want to know if you could find it in your heart to forgive me."

The long silence on the other end of the line seemed like an eternity. Would he scorn her? Would he rage at her hypocrisy? Would he . . . what was that she heard? It was a sob.

On a Saturday afternoon, six months later, I had the privilege of remarrying these two. It was a day they had waited for for so long they had forgotten they were waiting. My memory of the day is that when we weren't crying, we were laughing.

CHAPTER EIGHT
Keep on Laughing

—— GENESIS 18 ——

It is the hottest part of the day. Work is an impossibility, and sleep, the only respite. So Abraham sits in the shade at the entrance to his tent, drowsily watching the heat waves rise from the horizon.

Note that it is now Abraham who sits there, not Abram. It's the same man, but with a new name. God changed it earlier that year as Abraham turned ninety-nine (Gen 17:4-6). Names were very significant for Hebrews. A name was more than a designation; it signified an identity, even a destiny. To change a name was to exercise an awesome power over a person, for it meant a change in who that person was and in what he or she would do and become. God had exercised that power over Abraham. *Abram* means "exalted father." *Abraham* means "father of many." By changing his name, God set Abraham apart as his special servant with a special destiny—to be the father of a great nation, through which he would bless the earth. He did the same thing with Sarai, changing her name to Sarah (Gen 17:15-16). Both names meant "princess," but the renaming stressed that she belonged to God and what she would do—give birth to nations and kings.

The forge has been doing its work! In the twenty-four years since God first promised to give these two childless senior citizens a son, the wait has been purifying and shaping Abram and Sarai into Abraham and Sarah. Remember: from God's reckoning, at least as important as the thing we wait for is what we become as we wait. Faith and character are forged in delay. So is a marvelous sense of humor.

It's Abraham, not Abram, we see sitting drowsily at the entrance to his tent. He is nodding off to sleep when out of the corner of his eye he sees three men standing nearby. They seem to have appeared out of nowhere, and something strange stirs deep inside Abraham when he sees them, something like fear, but not quite. It's more like excitement and anticipation.

He rises immediately, his head suddenly clear, and rushes over to where they stand. Hospitality is a sacred duty for the Bedouin, so he bows low before them and speaks to the one who seems to be their leader:

> If I have found favor in your eyes, my lord, do not pass your servant by. Let a little water be brought, and then you may all wash your feet and rest under this tree. Let me get you something to eat, so you can be refreshed and then go on your way—now that you have come to your servant. (Gen 18:3-5)

The perfect host is the one who says, as each guest arrives, "I'm so glad *you* are finally here!" And when each leaves, "Must you go so soon?" Abraham is the perfect host. When they agree to stay and to accept his hospitality, he hurries into the tent and says to his wife, Sarah, "Quick, get three seahs of fine flower and knead it and bake some bread" (Gen 18:6). He then runs out to his herd, picks out one of his best, most tender calves and orders a servant to slaughter it and cook it. He then brings some curds and milk for his guests to enjoy as they wait for the bread and meat to cook.

The three men eat silently for a while as Abraham stands watching them, trying to understand the feeling he has in their presence. Then they speak, asking him where his wife, Sarah, is. Abraham says, "There, in the tent." Then the leader speaks, and Abraham knows the reason for his butterflies. This is no man, and no stranger; this is the One he had heard speak to him the year before, but had not seen. This is the One who promised him and Sarah a son. This is the Lord! "Then the LORD said, 'I will surely return to you about this time next year, and Sarah your wife will have a son' " (Gen 18:10).

Sarah heard him. As the men ate, Sarah, who must have had the same feeling about them as did Abraham, lay on the floor near the entrance of the tent eavesdropping on the conversation. She hears the man say, "Sarah your wife will have a son," and she has to stifle her reaction. She has heard that story before; for the last twenty-four years, to be exact. But now she is in her nineties, and Abraham is nearly one hundred years old. She has long since given up on the hope. It hurt for a while to wait and not to receive. Then the hurt turned to anger, and the anger to cold resignation. She is surprised at what she feels now. When she hears the seemingly empty promise again, it strikes her as . . . well, *funny!* "Sarah laughed to herself as she thought,

'After I am worn out and my master is old, will I now have this pleasure?' " (Gen 18:12).

She is still holding her hand over her mouth when the man talking to her husband speaks again. She might not have heard him had he not used her name again. He said, "Why did Sarah laugh and say, 'Will I really have a child, now that I am old?' " And before she can crawl away to the back of the tent and hide, he continues: "Is anything too hard for the LORD? I will return to you at the appointed time next year and Sarah will have a son." He has heard her thoughts! This is no ordinary man! Terrified at what is happening, she shouts from inside the tent, "I did not laugh." Without even turning in her direction, the stranger says, "Yes, you did laugh" (Gen 18:13-15).

Incongruity and Surprise

What is the meaning of Sarah's laugh?[1] Or, for that matter, what makes any of us laugh? What constitutes humor? This may come as a surprise to you, but philosophers of the stature of Aristotle, Bergson and Schopenhauer have debated this question and written books detailing their answers. Even the great Sigmund Freud, himself as "humorless as a chicken,"[2] wrote an essay entitled "Jokes and Their Relation to the Unconscious." A real side-splitter, I'm sure. Throughout all of the theories, two elements seem always to be present in what makes something funny: incongruity and surprise.

Incongruity is the juxtaposition of two or three apparently contradictory or unrelated ideas or situations. Surprise comes from the introduction of something into a scheme or story—an idea, an event, a person—that is totally unexpected and unanticipated. Incongruity and surprise are closely related, of course, and are sometimes indistinguishable from one another. Both capitalize on the twist, the unforeseeable. Both jolt us out of one mental attitude into another, which may be completely and even violently opposed to the first. It's incongruity and surprise that lie behind the humor of one-liners like Henny Youngman's: "Take my wife . . . please." Or Woody Allen's: "I don't believe in an afterlife, but I'm taking along an extra pair of underwear just in case." In an extended way, incongruity and surprise are the dynamics behind the comic success of Mark Twain's *A Connecticut Yankee in King Arthur's Court.*

Incongruity and surprise go together in humor. But—and this is the crucial point for us in understanding Sarah's laugh—it is possible to have humor that deals only in the incongruous and is completely without surprise. That is Sarah's humor. She can laugh at the preposterousness, the incongruity of an old bag having a baby, of having one foot in the grave and the other in a maternity ward. But that is all she can laugh at: its incongruity. She expects no surprises from God, no novelty, no violations of the world she has grown accustomed to living in and, as a result, her laugh can be only bitter and cynical. She can hear the Lord say, "Sarah, your wife, will have a son," and she can crack up in her bitterness. She cannot hear God say, "Is anything too hard for the LORD?" If she could, incongruity and surprise would come together, and she would really throw her head back and laugh as she has never laughed before—and she wouldn't cover her mouth when she did. She would be laughing and weeping at the same time.

A Prelude to Faith

Theologian Reinhold Niebuhr once preached a brilliant sermon on humor and faith.[3] He described humor as a "prelude to faith," meaning that it is our sense of the incongruous that can lead us to trust God. The same human faculty that enables us to laugh at an arrogant man slipping on a banana peel is what can open us up to faith. We laugh at the incongruity of the contrast between his arrogance and false dignity on the one hand, and the humiliation and indignity of his fall on the other. That kind of humor can serve us very well in the everyday occurrences of our lives. It helps us to stand outside of ourselves. It can help us avoid pretense and sham. It can be a guard against taking ourselves too seriously. If you have ever had a day in which everything was going wrong, and you were able, finally, to laugh at it all—at the incongruity of what you want and what you are actually getting—then you know what I mean. This kind of laughter has saved my marriage.

But let that same ability to stand outside of ourselves and to see the incongruous be extended out to the ultimate things of life, and suddenly the laughter stops. Because then we discover that we all are slipping on banana peels. For what is our position in the universe but incongruous? We aspire to eternity and slip on the banana peel of death. We aspire to greatness and slip on the banana peel of insignificance. Standing on earth, looking out at the universe, we can feel big. But standing out on the edge of the universe looking back at ourselves, we are dwarfed into nothingness. Pascal was thinking of this awkward incongruity when he described the universe as so large that "the centre is . . . everywhere, the circumference nowhere." What is man in all that? What can he be? Answers Pascal: He is "a Nothing in comparison with the Infinite, an All in comparison with the Nothing, a mean between nothing and everything."[4]

The Bible agrees. It asks the same questions:

O LORD, what is man that you care for him,

the son of man that you think of him?
Man is like a breath;
his days are like a fleeting shadow. (Ps 144:3-4)

Social, intellectual and economic distinctions among humans are meaningless when set against the monumental reality of death. The weak and poor know this. The powerful and rich kid themselves.

Lowborn men are but a breath,
the highborn are but a lie;
If weighed on a balance, they are nothing;
together they are only a breath. (Ps 62:9)

We are like the cartoon character Charlie Brown. Each year he tries to kick the football offered by Lucy. Each year she pulls it away just as he is about to kick it. Each year he swears he'll not try again, and each year he is duped into just one more attempt. In one of these episodes, Charlie Brown is taking the long run toward the ball. As always, he kicks into a blank space left by the ball she has jerked away. In the final frame, he is laying on his back, and Lucy is looking down into his face saying, "Your faith in human nature is an inspiration to all young people."

There is humor in the incongruity of Charlie Brown's trust and Lucy's deceit, humor in the disparity between what he desires and what he actually gets. But the humor becomes bitter when the football is a life with meaning, when it is eternal life, when it is significance in a universe that dwarfs not only each one of us, but even the planet on which we live.

It is in this sense that humor can be a prelude to faith. If it can help us to see the ultimate incongruity of our lives, and therefore the impossibility of us ever being more than a giant contradiction, a bad joke in ourselves, then it can open us up to faith.

God's Joke

When Sarah laughs, she is laughing the laugh of a cynic who will not try to kick the football one more time. She is laughing the laugh of despair that will not see anything but the ultimate incongruity of her life. Her long waiting has sapped her of her humor. Take surprise away from your sense of the incongruous, and all that remains is a bitter chuckle. That is why God's response to Sarah has such force. When he says to her, "Is anything too hard for the LORD?" he is inviting her to have a really good laugh and let surprise back into her life. He invites us to do the same. It is only when our sense of the incongruity of our lives meets God's great surprise of grace and promise that we are enabled to live our lives with the hilarity he intended. There's a version of pop psychology whose slogan is "I'm OK, You're OK." With the gospel, it is different: it is "I'm Not OK, You're Not OK, But It's OK!"

"Is anything too hard for God?" That is an overwhelming and shattering question. It demands an answer. Answer yes and the world is shut down, the universe is closed, and God is no longer God: benevolent, maybe; kindly and concerned, perhaps; but as powerless as we are in the face of our cosmic incongruity. Answer "No, there is nothing that is too hard for God," and you and the world are in his hands and the possibilities are endless. He is radically free to keep his promises, despite the odds against it.

But beware. When his surprise completes your incongruity, you had better be ready to be shaken out of your customary, stable, reliable but hopeless existence. Sarah will go through a pregnancy in her nineties, and worse, her son's adolescence when she is over one hundred! The question is, do we really want to believe that with God there is nothing that is impossible? For if we do believe that, then we can no longer be content to keep on living our lives as though business were normal. Wild and crazy things can happen and usually do.

As we wait, it is critical that we keep our sense of humor in the fullest meaning of that word. When laughter goes, so does hope. When God reaffirms his promise to Abraham and Sarah, he restores not only their faith, but their ability to laugh as well. One goes with the other. Only the laughers can believe. Only the believers can laugh. The only thing worse than waiting is waiting without laughing.

The Real McCoy

Let me tell you a very "humorous" story. It's about a seventy-two-year-old Baptist preacher named Charles McCoy.[5] McCoy was pastoring a Baptist church in Oyster Bay, New York, when at age seventy-two he was mandated by his denomination to retire. A lifelong bachelor, he had cared for his mother for as long as she lived. In his spare time he had earned seven university degrees, including two Ph.D.'s—one from Dartmouth, the other from Columbia. But now, at age seventy-two, he was being forced to retire from the ministry.

He was depressed. "I just lay on my bed thinking that my life's over, and I haven't really done anything yet. I've been pastor of this church for so many years and nobody really wants me much—what have I done for Christ? I've spent an awful lot of time working for degrees, but what does that count for? I haven't won very many to the Lord."[6]

A week later he met a Christian pastor from India, and on impulse asked him to preach in his church. After the service the Indian brother asked him matter-of-factly to return the favor.

Since he had preached for McCoy, would McCoy come to India and preach for him? McCoy told him that he was going to have to retire and move to a home for the elderly down in Florida. But the Indian insisted, informing McCoy that where he came from, people respected a man when his hair turns white. Would he come?

McCoy thought and prayed about it and decided he would. The members of his church were aghast. Dire predictions were made. The young chairman of his board of deacons summed up the attitude of the congregation when he asked, "What if you die in India?" I love McCoy's answer. He told him he reckoned "it's just as close to heaven from there as it is from here." He sold most of his belongings, put what was left in a trunk, and booked a one-way passage to India—his first trip ever out of the United States!

When he arrived in Bombay, he discovered to his horror that his trunk was lost. All he had were the clothes on his back, his wallet, his passport, and the address of missionaries in Bombay he had clipped from a missionary magazine when he left. He asked for directions, got on a streetcar and headed for their house. When he got there, he discovered that while he was on the streetcar his wallet and passport had been stolen! He went to the missionaries who welcomed him in, but who told him the man who had invited him to come to India was still in the U.S.A. and would probably remain there indefinitely.

What was he going to do now? they wanted to know. Unperturbed, McCoy told them he had come to preach and that he would try to make an appointment with the mayor of Bombay. They warned him that the mayor was very busy and important and that in all the years they had been missionaries there, they had never succeeded in getting an appointment with him. Nevertheless, McCoy set out for the mayor's office the next day—and he got in! When the mayor saw McCoy's business card, listing all his degrees, he reasoned that McCoy must not be merely a Christian pastor, but someone much more important. Not only did he get an appointment, but the mayor held a tea in his honor, attended by all of the big officials in Bombay! Old Dr. McCoy was able to preach to these leaders for half an hour. Among them was the director of India's West Point, the National Defense Academy at Poona. He was so impressed at what he heard that he invited McCoy to preach there.

Thus was launched, at age seventy-two, a brand new, sixteen-year ministry for Dr. Charles McCoy. Until he died at age eighty-eight, this dauntless old man circled the globe preaching the gospel. There is a church in Calcutta today because of his preaching and a thriving band of Christians in Hong Kong because of his faithful ministry. He never had more than enough money than to get him to the next place he was to go. He died one afternoon at a hotel in Calcutta, resting for a meeting he was to preach at that evening. He had indeed found himself as close to heaven there as he would have been at his church in Oyster Bay, New York, or in a retirement home in Florida. It was incongruous—an old man, waiting to die at age seventy-two, leaving everything he had ever known and preaching around the world. That's funny! But funnier still was the surprise of God's grace, completing the incongruity of this old man. May we all know this quality of humor in our lives as we wait!

Notes

[1]The seminal material for my thoughts here is from Frederick Buechner, *Telling the Truth: The Gospel as Tragedy, Comedy & Fairy Tale* (New York: Harper

and Row, 1977).

[2]A phrase borrowed from John Steinbeck.

[3]Reinhold Niebuhr, "Humour and Faith," *Twenty Centuries of Great Preaching*, eds. Clyde E. Fant and William M. Pinson, vol. 10 (Waco, Tex.: Word, 1971), pp. 373-82.

[4]Blaise Pascal, *Pensées*, The Great Books (Chicago, Ill.: University of Chicago Press, 1952), p. 181.

[5]Franklin Graham, with Jeanette Lockerbie, Bob Pierce, *This One Thing I Do* (Waco, Tex.: Word, 1983), pp. 115-21.

[6]Ibid, p. 117.

I *know her well, this wife of mine. I've stood beside* Lauretta at the birth of our four children. I can often tell what she will say before she says it. Her moods, her profile, the way her eyebrows arch when she talks seriously, her inability to remember the punch line of a joke, the way she bounces up on her toes when she runs, her icy feet on the back of my thighs when we get in bed—I know these like I know myself.

But there are times when it is as though I'm seeing her for the first time. Like the night we sat up late and talked. A warm rain was falling outside. The air was heavy with the smell of freshly mown summer grass. I don't recall the subject of the conversation, but I'll never forget how the mystery of her washed over me. Where did she come from? How on earth did I ever end up with her? Who is she, really? God! I'm glad to be with her! She will always be Eve to this Adam.

I didn't plan on her. In all the years I waited for her, I never once asked God to give me this particular woman. Sometimes I look at the knuckles on my right hand. There is no sign of the damage I did to them so many years ago as I smashed them into my dashboard out of frustration over a lost love.

I thank God for all the times I've prayed for silver and he's said no—and made me wait so he could give me gold instead.

CHAPTER NINE
Partners in Waiting

—— GENESIS 18:16-33 ——

In 1952, a doctoral student at Princeton asked, "What is there left in the world for original dissertation research?" Visiting lecturer Albert Einstein answered, "Find out about prayer. Somebody must find out about prayer."[1]

But that is the problem. How do you "find out" about prayer? Prayer is a mystery, and its mystery is compounded by the fact that it does not lend itself to scientific research. A fundamental assumption of scientific inquiry is that the thing under scrutiny must be studied objectively. Whether flowers or sunspots or cancer cells, it is essential to the scientific method for the observer to keep his or her distance from the thing being studied, to achieve what we like to call "objectivity." The observer is the subject; the thing being studied is the object.

But God will never be for us an object to study. He is a subject who addresses us and to whom we must respond. He cannot be studied; he must be engaged. Our relationship to God is not that of subject to object, but of subject to subject; or, as Martin Buber puts it, an I to a Thou.

As with God, the best way to find out about prayer is by praying, not by standing back and thinking about it. We see this so clearly in the prayer conversation Abraham has with God in Genesis 18. The prayer there is an example of prayer at its deepest— a wrestling, an encounter, an engagement of almost violent proportions between this man and his Lord. It is also a picture of the kind of prayer most critical for those who wait. For to be caught up in acute waiting is often to have no other recourse but to pray as Abraham did.

Prayer—A Mystery and a Grace

The first thing we see about prayer in this encounter is that it is God who takes the initiative. Prayer is both a mystery and a grace. As with God's gracious promise, so with the gift of prayer. In both, it is God who makes the first move. As the story opens, God has just appeared to Abraham in the form of three angels and reaffirmed through them his promise to give him and Sarah a son. The miraculous child will come the next year. Now the angels, who look like ordinary men, are leaving Abraham's tent to travel to the wicked city of Sodom. Abraham is walking a short distance with them. As they walk, the Lord is thinking:

Shall I hide from Abraham what I am about to do? Abraham will surely become a great and powerful nation, and all nations on earth will be blessed through him. For I have chosen him, so that he will direct his children and his household after him to keep the way of the LORD by doing what is right and just,

136

so that the LORD will bring about for Abraham what he has promised him.

Then the LORD said, "The outcry against Sodom and Gomorrah is so great and their sin so grievous that I will go down and see if what they have done is as bad as the outcry that has reached me. If not, I will know." (Gen 18:17-21)

God takes the initiative in prayer. He does this by showing us something of himself—who he is, what he has done, or what he plans to do. For some of us it is a simple hunger to know more of God. For others it is the pain of circumstances that pushes us to pray, the reading of Scripture or the preaching of God's Word. Whichever, it is God taking the initiative to show us something of himself that draws us into prayer. With Abraham it is inside information: God plans to investigate the charges against Sodom and Gomorrah and, if necessary, destroy these two vile cities.

God accomplishes two things this way. The first is that he prods Abraham to approach his high calling with an appropriately high sense of responsibility. The utter destruction of Sodom and Gomorrah will be an object lesson for Abraham. He wants him to tell his children: "Look: this is what happens to those who sin unrepentantly. Remember it. Live your life accordingly."

It is worth noting here that God does not shrink from using fear as a way to make us get serious about our faith. C. S. Lewis observed that it is better to serve God out of love and gratitude. That is the high road of service. But failing that, a healthy fear of the consequences of not serving him will do for starters. Better to serve him from less than the best of motives than *not* to serve him for the best of motives. Better the low road than no road at all.

It was Pascal who noted the tragedy of fearing what we should not, and not fearing what we should. So many of us fall into that trap. We fear opening our lives to Christ when our fear should be precisely the opposite. We are like the little girl who had been reading so many nursery rhymes and fairy tales that they were beginning to get mixed up in her mind. Her bedtime story on Saturday night had been *The Three Little Pigs.* The Sunday-school lesson the next morning was from Revelation 3:20, about inviting Jesus to come and live in her heart. When asked by the teacher if she wanted to let Jesus come into her heart, she said indignantly, "Not by the hair of my chinny-chin-chin."

A Holy Shock

The second thing God accomplishes with Abraham is to draw him into prayer. Abraham is shocked by what he hears, for his nephew Lot lives in Sodom! What will happen to him? Verse 22 says: "The men turned away and went toward Sodom, but Abraham remained standing before the LORD."

There is good reason to believe that that verse, as it now stands, may not be what was originally written. There is an ancient Hebrew text of the Old Testament called the Masoretic text. Among other things, it preserves a record of the various textual changes that have taken place in the Old Testament Scriptures. The Masoretic text says that the original sentence was "But the LORD remained standing before Abraham," and suggests that it was changed by pious scribes because the original sounded irreverent to them. Perhaps they reasoned: "Someone must have goofed to write down that the Almighty God would remain standing before a mere man, awaiting a response." So they changed it—thus says the usually reliable Masoretic text. If that is indeed the case, then it is clear that God has laid all his plans out before Abraham and is now waiting for Abraham to respond, to speak back—in other words, to pray. It is as though God is provoking Abraham to pray: "Here's what I'm going to do, Abraham. Now what do you think of that?"

Whether or not the line we have before us is the original or a change, prayer is what God's announcement elicits in Abraham. It draws him—no, it jolts him—into prayer. That is so often the way God gets you and me to pray. He jolts us. He breaks into our lives without explanation or warning. It may be in that telephone call that shatters us or that letter that disturbs us. It may be in the hurtful words we hear from a spouse or a friend. Perhaps it is the loss of a job or the failure of health. Suddenly we are faced with something that challenges our deepest securities, knocks away all of our props, or violates everything we have ever believed to be true about God.

When things like that happen to us, we can rest assured that God has taken the initiative with us in prayer. And those aren't the only ways. He can also initiate prayer by overwhelming us with his grace and kindness. But that is not how God is now doing it with Abraham, and I know that is not how God is doing it with many of you right now. Right now you are jolted and stopped dead in your tracks by what has happened to you.

Wrestling with God

When God jolts us this way, it is because he wants us to wrestle with him in prayer. Abraham has just heard God say that he is going to destroy a city that has in it his nephew Lot as a citizen. How can he do such a thing?

Then Abraham approached him and said: "Will you sweep away the righteous with the wicked? What if there are fifty

139

righteous people in the city? Will you really sweep it away and not spare the place for the sake of fifty righteous people in it? Far be it from you to do such a thing—to kill the righteous with the wicked, treating the righteous and the wicked alike. Far be it from you! Will not the Judge of all the earth do right?" (Gen 18:23-25)

Abraham is perplexed and bewildered at what he has heard from God, so he expostulates and accuses him—he does the next thing to attacking his integrity. That is the way it is with faith and waiting—it is a wrestling with bewilderment and perplexity. G. Campbell Morgan writes, "Faith is the answer to a question; and, therefore, it is out of work when there is no question to ask." If there is no perplexity, there is no faith. How else could it be with a finite human trying to understand and trust an infinite God?

When I was a young candidate for ordination to the ministry of the Presbyterian Church, I was required to come under what is called the "care" of the presbytery. That meant I was to be under the guidance and observation of the elders of the presbytery for two years, to determine if I was fit for the ministry. Part of the process of coming under care is to appear before the entire presbytery and give a statement of faith, along with a brief, autobiographical sketch, telling them why you want to go into the ministry and how you heard God's call. Three of us appeared before the presbytery that day. I'll never forget what one candidate told the assembly. To explain why he felt God was calling him into the ministry, he said, "When I was eighteen years old and a senior in high school, I wrote down all the questions I had about God. There were exactly one hundred. The last four years of college have been spent finding answers to these questions. I have successfully answered all one hundred. Now I would like to become a pastor and tell people the answers to my questions."

The presbytery was stunned. During the time for questioning, a pastor with a very gentle spirit stood up and asked the young candidate, "Did I hear you say that you at one time had one hundred questions about God? And that now you have answered them all and no longer have any questions?" The candidate answered, "Yes, that is correct." The pastor thanked him and sat down. When it came time to vote on whether to bring us under care, the three of us were asked to leave the room. After a long wait, we were brought back in and told that we had been accepted. The fellow with no more questions was accepted with one stipulation, however—that he seek psychological counseling!

He needed more than counseling; he needed conversion. If our faith in God does not leave us somewhat bewildered and perplexed, then we have domesticated him, and we no longer believe in God but in an intellectual system. Beware that you not handle holy things and hear holy things so much that your hands and ears are cauterized and you no longer are burned and jolted at what you touch and hear!

It's easy for Christians to become like the people who once greeted President Franklin Roosevelt at a gala ball. Tired of shaking hands and smiling his big smile and saying all of the usual inanities at such occasions, Roosevelt tried doing something outrageous. Convinced that no one was listening anyway, he greeted each person by saying, "I murdered my grandmother this morning." Everyone he met smiled vacuously and said things like: "Wonderful!" "Lovely!" "Keep up the good work!" One diplomat was listening, however. He leaned over and whispered in Roosevelt's ear, "I'm sure she had it coming to her!"[2] If you are not shocked from time to time by what God does and says, then you have not been listening to him.

He's Always Better than We Thought

To wait on God and to pray is to wrestle with bewilderment and perplexity. But it is God himself who brings on the bewilderment and perplexity. He does it that he might cause us to so encounter him and wrestle with him that we come to know him as we never have before. It is his way of making us come to know more deeply his goodness and mercy.

After Abraham pours out his questioning indignation, God says to him:

If I find fifty righteous people in the city of Sodom, I will spare the whole place for their sake.

Abraham calms down a bit and then asks, a bit more humbly:

Now that I have been so bold as to speak to the Lord, though I am nothing but dust and ashes, what if the number of the righteous is five less than fifty? Will you destroy the whole city because of five people?

Abraham, the sly fox, has engaged in a little bargaining legerdemain. A lot more than five people in Sodom are wicked—there are thousands! He tries to make it sound like God is picking at nits. But the Lord ignores this and says, "If I find forty-five there, I will not destroy it."

And so it goes. What about forty? God says that would keep him from wiping out the place. What about thirty? That too. And twenty? Yes. Ten? Absolutely (Gen 18:26-33).

Where does this wrestling take Abraham? It takes him to the place where he discovers God to be better than he ever even imagined! "God is not only better than our fears," says G. Campbell Morgan, "he is better than our hopes, better than the very best we had dared to suppose. We stop at ten. God takes care of the one." The worst thing we can ever do in our wait for God is to run away from the struggle of faith and fall into bitterness. It is always worth our while to hold fast to God in prayer in the midst of perplexity. For he created the perplexity and wills that we wrestle it through until the end. When we do, we will discover God to have been far better than we ever knew him to be, and we ourselves will be changed. For as the numbers dropped from fifty to ten, Abraham's faith went up inversely.

Wrestle with God! That's what Jacob, Abraham's yet-to-be-born grandson, will do one night years later by the River Jabbok. On his way to attempt reconciliation with his estranged brother, Esau, he meets a stranger with whom he wrestles all night. It's nearly dawn, and the two have struggled to a standstill. Sometime in the night of wrestling, Jacob becomes aware that he is wrestling with more than a man. So when his opponent says, "Let me go, for it is daybreak," Jacob answers: "I will not let you go until you bless me." The man agrees to bless him. His blessing? He changes his name to Israel, which means, "he struggles with God." The man disappears and Jacob realizes the stupendous thing that has happened. He gives a name to the place where they wrestled, calling it Peniel, meaning "face of God," because "I saw God face to face, and yet my life was spared" (Gen 32:22-30). His wrestling turned out to be a face-to-face meeting with the Almighty himself. In the Bible, Israel is the chief name for God's people. By definition, to belong to God is to be a "God-wrestler"!

A good wrestler is tenacious. The Gospel writer Luke introduces one of Jesus' parables on prayer with the words, "Then Jesus told this diciples a parable to show them that they should always pray and not give up." At the end of the parable, Jesus concludes with the words, "When the Son of Man comes, will he find faith on earth?" When he returns, will he find his people still persistent and tenacious in prayer? (Lk 18:1-8).

Modern Christians are afflicted with a "zap mentality." It's the idea that unless God "zaps" us immediately in response to our prayers, unless he does something that is immediately accessible to our five senses, then nothing has happened. The "zap mentality" approaches prayer as an experiment in a chemistry lab— you mix the substances and wait for the reaction. If there is no reaction, then the experiment didn't work. To change the metaphor, praying is like farming. No farmer plants a seed and then stands over it waiting to see if anything happened. He knows the seeds must be planted and watered and cared for and waited on over time before they bring a harvest.

It is persistence and tenacity of this kind that gets us through the troughs and low spots in our wait for God. How we deal with the low spots in the wait is crucial to the outcome of our wait. C. S. Lewis underscores this in his imaginary correspondence between two devils in *The Screwtape Letters*. Addressing his nephew Wormwood on the subject of temptation, the devil Screwtape gives some shrewd advice on how the "Enemy" (God) works with humans. He observes that at the beginning of our walk of faith, God often gives us powerful intimations of his presence. But that state of affairs usually doesn't last for long. There is a good reason.

> He leaves the creature to stand on its own two legs—to carry from the will alone duties which have lost all relish. It is during such trough periods, much more than during the peak periods, that it is growing into the creature He wants it to be. Hence

the prayers offered in the state of dryness are those that please Him best. . . . He cannot 'tempt' virtue as we can to vice. He wants them to learn to walk and must therefore take away His hand; and if only the will to walk is really there He is pleased even with their stumbles. Do not be deceived, Wormwood. Our cause is never more in danger than when a human, no longer desiring, but still intending, to do our Enemy's will, looks round a universe from which every trace of Him seems to have vanished, and asks why he has been forsaken, and still obeys.[3]

We are forged in the wait. The prayers we pray while in the forge are critical to the men and women we become.

A Living God

Finally, we learn in this prayer of Abraham's that the God to whom we pray is a living God. That is to say that he is actually affected by our prayers. When the Bible says that God is high above, it does not mean he is above us as one removed, but above us as one who is the Lord, who directs our lives. It is as Lord that he is involved in our lives. It is as Lord that he is affected by what happens to us. The characteristic adjective the Greeks used to describe the gods was *apatheia,* from *a,* meaning "no," and *patheia,* meaning "feeling." "No feeling": that's what the gods were like. They were unmoved and unaffected by human misery. Some Greeks, like Plato, reasoned that if a god was moved by something smaller than him, he would be less than the thing that moved him.

But nothing could be further from the biblical doctrine of God. Listen to what God says through the prophet Hosea to the people of Israel. Even though his people have sinned grievously against him, he must say:

145

How can I give you up? . . . How can I hand you over, Israel? . . . My heart is changed within me; all my compassion is aroused. (Hos 11:8-9)

God tells Israel that he is moved by his love for them. He is affected by their haplessness and self-destruction.

Because our God is a living God and is therefore affected by us, he also responds to our prayers. He may really change what he was going to do as a result of our prayers. In his sovereign lordship over our lives, he grants to the prayer of faith a power to which he consents to submit. He works upon us by his grace and allows us to work on him by our faith. He takes the initiative with us in prayer and invites us to do the same with him when we pray. In prayer, God relinquishes some of his sovereign power to us, and there are some things that he simply will not do until we pray for them to happen.

My wife's aunt Ione is a living example of this. After her seventh cancer surgery, the doctors sewed her up and gave up. She had two months to live, they said. That was twenty-nine years ago! Ione was ready to die then: she had accepted the verdict, she was at peace with God and had suffered so much she rather wanted it all to end, anyway. She prayed no prayers to live; she wanted to die and go to be with Jesus. But her father, Henry, had other ideas. He had definitely not accepted it and wouldn't hear of her talk about dying and going to heaven. He wanted her alive! And he pestered and wrestled with God until he healed her.

God's will would not have been thwarted one bit had she died. She would have gone to be with him and that would have been good. God would have triumphed over the evil of cancer in that way. And, I might add, she will still die some day just as Lazarus did after Jesus raised him from the dead. But God was waiting

146

for a Henry Soltau to say to him with a holy impertinence: "Far be it from you to do such a thing! Shame! Show your justice and love and heal my daughter!" So he did just that. God didn't have to do it, he was under no necessity, but he wanted to let Henry affect him. Thus was his will done by responding to the prayer of a distraught father. Either way—by death or by healing—God's will would be done. But the living God was waiting for someone to lay hold of him and pray the prayer of faith so he could show to those who would see that he is just and kind and loving.[4]

He was looking for a partner, not a "yes man." A "yes man" submits to God with stoic resignation. There is no joy, no transformation, just a grim acceptance of the inevitable. A partner can finally submit after great wrestlings, and with great joy. He can embrace God's will, as he embraced him in the struggle. We have not because we ask not!

That is not to say that we will always get what we ask just the way we ask for it. Often God will say no to our specific requests so that he might say yes to the hope that lies behind the requests, and give us something far better. As Luther phrased it, "We pray for silver, but God often gives us gold instead."[5] The Puritan Richard Sibbes wrote that God will sometimes heal us not by healing, but by leaving "infirmities to cure enormities."[6] The prayer that wrestles with the living God has the faith to believe in the end that even the apparent silence of God is the silence of his higher thoughts and that his no is spoken that he might give us a more resounding yes.

There is a lovely poem which speaks to this wonderfully. It was reputedly written by a young soldier who received massive and permanently debilitating injuries in the Civil War. He lived as a cripple the rest of his days, wrestling and waiting for God to show

147

his face, his purpose in it all. At the end of his strugglings, he wrote this:

I asked for strength that I might achieve;

I was made weak that I might obey.

I asked for health that I might do greater things;

I was given infirmity that I might do better things.

I asked for riches that I might be happy;

I was given poverty that I might be wise.

I asked for power that I might have the praise of men;

I was given weakness that I might feel the need of God.

I asked for all things that I might enjoy life;

I was given life that I might enjoy all things.

I have received nothing I asked for, all that I hoped for.

My prayer is answered.

Such sentiments can be expressed, not at the beginning of our struggle with God, but only at the end. It is a precious intimacy with the heart of God that can see through all of our disappointments the tender and loving hand of God at work for our good. That intimacy comes only after years spent in dialog with him, a dialog that is sometimes quiet and peaceful and sometimes wrenching and devastating. But through it all there is the same loving God, no matter how we feel him to be at the moment— adversary or advocate, mother or father, friend or enemy. Through it all he is at work for our good, and his victory over us will be also his victory in us when the wrestling is over.

Notes

[1]Cited in *Leadership Journal,* Winter 1983, p. 43.

[2]Cited in *Parables, Etc.,* October 1984 (Saratoga, Calif.: Saratoga Press), p. 5.

[3]C. S. Lewis, *The Screwtape Letters* (New York: Macmillan, 1944), p. 47.

[4]The best discussion on this subject I have ever read is in a book that is also the best on prayer that I have ever read:, P. T. Forsyth, *The Soul of Prayer* (Grand Rapids, Mich.: Eerdmans, 1916), see especially pp. 81-92.

[5]As quoted in Donald Bloesch, *The Struggle of Prayer* (New York: Harper and Row, 1980), p. 91.

[6]Ibid., p. 93.

T*he thought comes to Rick at the oddest moments.* Or is it the voice of God? A man of deep and tenacious faith, he thinks it is the latter. When a boy, he lost an eye in an accident with an air rifle. The voice asks: "Rick, would you give up the other eye if I asked for it?" He always answers, "Yes, Lord, I think so." But what kind of God would ask for something like that? How could there possibly be any love in that kind of request? The only way to find out would be to obey and then wait.

CHAPTER TEN
Faith's
Ultimate Test

—— GENESIS 22:1-19 ——

The American Banking Association once sponsored a two-week training program to help tellers detect counterfeit bills. The program was unique—never during the two-week training did the tellers even look at a counterfeit bill, nor did they listen to any lectures concerning the characteristics of counterfeit bills or denouncing the manufacture of counterfeit bills. All they did for two weeks was handle authentic currency, hour after hour and day after day, until they were so familiar with the true that they could not possibly be fooled by the false.

That is also the biblical approach to dealing with spiritual counterfeits. The idea is to become so familiar with the real thing, by meditating on it, praying about it and acting it out in everyday life, that the counterfeit can be recognized immediately. The story we are about to look at serves that function for a waiting faith.

It shows faith boiled down to its essence, its barest outlines. Meditate on this story, and you handle the real thing of faith, the genuine article. Ponder it long enough and well enough and you will be able to spot a counterfeit a mile away.

This story is significant for another reason. It happens near the end of Abraham's saga. God has kept his promise and given him the son for whom he had waited so long. The rest of his promise will come later, in the centuries after Abraham's death. Only then will God make him a great nation and bless the world through his offspring. For now he and Sarah have only their son Isaac, and that is enough. He is the down payment for the rest of God's promise; all the rest is contained in him. There is a lot more to wait for, but for all practical purposes the waiting is over. Abraham and Sarah are home free. Thank God, no more waiting!

Not quite. God has a surprise for the unsuspecting Abraham. He asks him to do the unthinkable—sacrifice Isaac as a burnt offering!

> Some time later God tested Abraham. He said to him, "Abraham!" "Here I am," he replied. Then God said, "Take your son, your only son, Isaac, whom you love, and go to the region of Moriah. Sacrifice him there as a burnt offering on one of the mountains I will tell you about." (Gen 22:1-2)

This is more than man can take. Throughout Abraham's story we have watched him learn how to wait. We have seen the forge at work in his life: In the delay between God's promise and its fulfillment, his faith and his character have been shaped and purified. The process has been slow and painful, but thorough. A great man has emerged, the promise has been kept. Isn't that enough? Have you ever asked the same question yourself? Aren't you finished with me yet, Lord? When will this be over? How much more does he think I can take? Why this, now?

A Pure Faith

The story says simply that God did it to test Abraham. No other explanation. He wasn't trying to tempt him to do evil, because God doesn't do that sort of thing (Jas 1:13). He was testing him to confirm what he was made of, to "prove" the quality of the work that had been done in the forge in all those years of waiting. What is the work of the forge? It is the purification of a man or a woman's faith. What is faith? When boiled down to its essence, to have faith is to take God at his word and to entrust yourself to it totally.

That is certainly what is involved here for Abraham. God had promised to give Abraham a son. And he had kept his promise. Why ask him now to sacrifice his son? Because Abraham, and you and I, are to trust God's Word, not the way we perceive he is going to keep that word. For Abraham, and for all of us, the temptation is always to trust in Isaac rather than to trust in God. To be sure, God gave Isaac as the fulfillment of his promise. But God can take Isaac away and still keep his promise. We must never trust in the Isaacs of our lives, but only in the God who gives the Isaacs. He can take them away if he so wills, and remain faithful even in the taking away. The great betrayal of faith is to trust in the gift instead of the giver of the gift.

Centuries later, God forced the descendants of Abraham and Isaac to wander in the desert for forty years. They lived from day to day by the hand of God. He caused them to be hungry and then fed them with manna. Moses explained to Israel God's rationale for this. It was

to humble you and to test you in order to know what was in

your heart, whether or not you would keep his commands, . . .
to teach you that man does not live on bread alone but on
every word that comes from the mouth of the LORD. (Deut
8:2-3)

Why did they have to wait so many years to enter into God's
promised land? The purpose of the wait was to teach them that
it was not God's manna that kept them alive, but God's word of
promise.

Becoming and being a Christian is the simplest and hardest
thing possible. It is simple because it is not complicated; there
are no elaborate doctrines or secrets to learn. All that is required
is that we take Jesus at his word completely. But that is the hard
part. That simple thing is the hardest thing possible for a human
being to do. It is so hard that Jesus says it can be done only by
the miracle of God's grace in the new birth (Jn 3:3).

Martin Luther said, "The only saving faith is that which casts
itself on God for life and death." Because faith casts itself on
God's Word for life or death, it then trusts God's Word in life or
death, in the face of all that would contradict it. "What you gonna
do when the river overflows?" asks the old poem. Faith answers,

I'm gonna sit on the porch and watch her go.
What you gonna do when the hogs all drown?
I'm gonna wish I lived on higher ground.
What you gonna do when the cow floats away?
I'm gonna throw in after her a bale of hay.
What you gonna do with the water in the room?
I'm gonna sweep her out with a sedge-straw broom.
What you gonna do when the cabin leaves?
I'm gonna climb on the roof and straddle the eaves.
What you gonna do when your hold gives way?

I'm gonna say, "Howdy, Lord! It's judgment day."
That is a pure faith. When life gets whittled down, faith doesn't. It begins trusting God's Word and ends doing the same.

A Powerful Faith

A pure faith is a powerful faith. When God is simply taken at his word and nothing else, faith takes on tenacity and strength. It can stand when all else fails. Because it is founded on God's Word alone, it is not shaken when external supports and evidences are removed. It just keeps on believing. It can say with Job, who was certainly deprived of all external assurances, "Though he slay me, yet will I hope in him" (Job 13:15). Thus Abraham sets out, trusting God's Word:

> Early the next morning Abraham got up and saddled his donkey. He took with him two of his servants and his son Isaac. When he had cut enough wood for the burnt offering, he set out for the place God had told him about. On the third day Abraham looked up and saw the place in the distance. (Gen 22:3-4)

Abraham's faith has great tenacity and power. God commands him to do this awful thing and, even though stupefied, he gets up early the next morning and starts traveling to a mountain that God says he will tell him about (Gen 22:2b). *Will* tell him about! It is one thing to hear the awful command, and to get up and have it done right away, without time to think too much about it. It is another thing to have to travel to an unknown place with time to spare. Abraham will travel three long days before he gets to the place where he will do this horrible deed. He will have three long days to ponder the will of God and the trustworthiness of his Word. He will have three long days to consider the alternatives. Then he will be required to take the long hike to the top of Mount Moriah, there to build an altar, all the time concealing from his beloved son, whom he plans to sacrifice, what he is going to do.

> As the two of them went on together, Isaac spoke up and said to his father Abraham, "Father?" "Yes, my son?" Abraham replied. "The fire and wood are here," Isaac said, "but where is the lamb for the burnt offering?" (Gen 22:6-7)

Agony! Trusting Isaac asks his stunned father where they will get the lamb for the sacrifice. What can he possibly say? God is giving Abraham every opportunity to opt out of faith. But Abraham's faith has great power and tenacity because it has great purity. It is built not on keeping Isaac, but on the trustworthiness of the one who gave him Isaac. Having learned to wait to receive the promise, Abraham can now let go of it. It has been said that faith is not believing something regardless of the evidence, but doing something regardless of the consequences. So Abraham answers his son:

> "God himself will provide the lamb for the burnt offering, my son." And the two of them went on together. (Gen 22:8)

It is not that God is a sadist who likes to dangle us over the abyss. He isn't a bully who wants to cow us into submission by constantly holding over us the possibility that he may one day take from us the things and people we most dearly love. It is just that none of the things we love is worthy of our complete trust. One day, in death, everything will be taken away from us: spouse, children, home, health, car, career—everything. Then all we will have will be God and his promise. But that is all we ever have. Our trust should never be in what God gives us, but in the God who gives. That is why Moses prayed, "Teach us to number our days aright, that we may gain a heart of wisdom" (Ps 90:12). God asks what he asks of Abraham, and all of us, mercifully. He desires not to tear from us our loves, but to push us back to our life—him.

The test of Abraham's faith, as for ours, is always the question: "Is there anything I could lose that would make me lose my trust in God?" It is a severe question, and one that none of us can answer ahead of time with any confidence. But we can pray that God will give us faith as we meet each test. And he will, for he tests us, not that we might fail, but that we might emerge pure and victorious.

The Foundation of Faith

We can also build our faith on a good foundation now. The foundation of faith is a firm conviction regarding three things about God—his perfect love, wisdom and power. Like a three-legged stool, no combination of two will do. There must be all three for faith to stand. A strong faith believes that God wills only what is best for us (his love), that he knows what is best for us (his wisdom), and that he is able to do what is best for us (his power). This was the foundation of Abraham's strong faith. The writer to the Hebrews said of Abraham:

> By faith Abraham, when God tested him, offered Isaac as a sacrifice. He who had received the promises was about to sacrifice his one and only son, even though God had said to him, "It is through Isaac that your offspring will be reckoned." Abraham reasoned that God could raise the dead, and figuratively speaking, he did receive Isaac back from death. (Heb 11:17-19)

Whatever God was up to, no matter how inscrutable, Abraham's strong faith believed it proceeded from his perfect love, wisdom

159

and power. Whatever it took for God to keep his promise, he believed God would do it. So he walked up Moriah to do the crazy thing God required.

God did not disappoint him.

When they reached the place God had told him about, Abraham built an altar there and arranged the wood on it. He bound his son Isaac and laid him on the altar, on top of the wood. Then he reached out his hand and took the knife to slay his son. But the angel of the LORD called out to him from heaven, "Abraham! Abraham!" "Here I am," he replied. "Do not lay a hand on the boy," he said. "Do not do anything to him. Now I know that you fear God, because you have not withheld from me your son, your only son." Abraham looked up and there in a thicket he saw a ram caught by its horns. He went over and took the ram and sacrificed it as a burnt offering instead of his son. (Gen 22:9-13)

On their way up the mountain, Isaac had asked Abraham where the lamb was they were going to sacrifice. Abraham said something that at first sounded like a merciful fiction. He said, "God himself will provide the lamb." But he wasn't lying. He believed that God would indeed provide whatever was necessary for God to demonstrate his perfect love, power and wisdom. Just how he would do it would be a surprise, but that is part of the passion of faith. God's methods are his business. Our business is to wait and see. "We do not see the answer," wrote P. T. Forsyth; "we trust the Answerer. We do not gain the victory; we are united with the Victor."[1] Abraham even names the place on the mountain, "The LORD Will Provide" (Gen 22:14). Wonderful! The same God who tests is also the God who provides. So often we don't want the test, we just want the provision. But if we are to have the

provision, we must undergo the test. "The LORD Will Provide"—
that is the name of the mountain on which every strong faith is
built. To confess that no matter what the Lord provides is to
confess that you believe he is perfect in his love, his power and
his wisdom.

The Key to a Strong Faith

The key to a strong faith is a close fellowship with God. When
we know intimately the God in whose word we trust, it becomes
easier to trust him when we have no other assurances but his
word. It is easy to see that this intimacy was the case with Abraham. Each time God says, "Abraham," he answers immediately,
"Here I am." That is a biblical way of expressing the quick and
ready obedience of a servant who knows his master well. And
well he might. He had spent twenty-four long years before Isaac's
birth becoming acquainted with this God's faithfulness and love.
He had the benefit of the years that had passed since his son's
birth to see in Isaac a daily, living reminder of God's faithfulness.
Abraham knew intimately the one in whom he trusted.

Abraham was like the young sailor in a story that was the
delight of Robert Louis Stevenson. Waves crashed over the ship
as it labored along the rocky coast. The danger in the air was
palpable. One sailor, toiling below the water line, could contain
himself no longer. In a panic, he stumbled up the stairs into the
control room where he stood frozen in terror, watching the captain grapple with the controls as he fought to steer the huge ship
through the rocks to open water. The captain looked over his
shoulder at the scared sailor and smiled. The sailor smiled back
and went back down below deck to tell the crew that everything
was going to be all right. When they asked him how he knew,

he said, "I have seen the face of the captain, and he smiled at me."

Abraham had spent years looking into the face of God and had seen his smile often enough to trust him when he couldn't see it. That is what a lifetime of waiting, in close fellowship with God, does for you. There are no shortcuts to that kind of trust. It comes only out of a reservoir of faith that has been fed by years of experience. And there is simply no substitute for the ups and downs of experience. I read of a young man who had just been appointed to the presidency of a bank at the tender age of thirty-two. The promotion was far beyond his wildest dreams and very frightening to him, so he went to the venerable old chairman of the board to ask for advice on how to be.

"What is the most important thing for me to do as a new president?" he asked the older man.

"Right decisions," was the gentleman's terse answer.

The young man thought about that for a moment, and said, "Thank you very much; that is very helpful. But can you be a bit more specific? How do I make good decisions?"

The wise old man answered, "Experience."

Exasperated, the young president said, "But that is why I'm here. I don't have the experience I need to make right decisions. How do I get experience?"

"Wrong decisions," came the old man's reply.

Spiritual maturity doesn't necessarily come with age, but it rarely comes without it. You learn to live by faith by living by faith. You grow by growing. The pain of living life is that you get little or no practice at it before you're born. As Garrison Keillor put it, "Life isn't a vicarious experience. You get it figured out and then one day life happens to you. You prepare yourself for grief and loss, arrange your ballast and then the wave swamps the boat."[2] Or, as George Bernard Shaw answered when asked how he acquired his marvelous oratorical abilities: "I learned to speak as men learn to skate or cycle, by doggedly making a fool out of myself until I got used to it."

But that's OK with God. Because this life is a time of preparation, of growth, of challenge and refinement. It is a forge. Martin Luther's words are an encouragement to all of us who wait through life:

> This life, therefore, is not righteousness, but growth in righteousness; not health, but healing; not being, but becoming; not rest, but exercise. We are not yet what we shall be, but we are growing toward it. The process is not yet finished, but it is going on. This is not the end but it is the road. All does not yet gleam in glory, but all is being purified.

A faith like Abraham's comes only through years of experience. There are, however, things we can do to enrich that experience. A life of prayer, meditation on the Holy Scriptures and the fellowship and worship of the church are chief. In fact they are critical. These things are to our faith what a look at the captain was to the frightened sailor. Prayer, Bible study, worship and fellowship in the Christian community, the Church, are definitely not "one-shot" experiences. Their value is cumulative, not instantaneous.

The letters to the editor section of a newspaper printed a letter complaining about the sermons the writer heard each week in his church. He figured that he had heard nearly 1500 sermons in a lifetime of church attendance, but could remember what was said in only two or three. He proposed that the sermon served no good purpose and should be discarded. A fury of protest followed. But the best word came from a man who wrote: "As near as I can tell, I have eaten nearly 55,000 meals in my fifty years on this planet. I can remember what I ate in only a few of them. I would give up eating, but I have the distinct impression that I would soon be dead if I did." The power of prayer, the Word of God, the fellowship and worship of the church are food to us. These exercises may not be memorable, but they are crucial to the nourishment of our life with God.

Not enough can be said about the importance of the fellowship of the church for those who wait, especially those who wait in "Isaac experiences." Sometimes the love of fellow Christians is the next best thing to the Lord himself coming down out of heaven to give comfort. It's usually his method of choice. Like the little boy who was awakened at 3:00 A.M. by a nightmare. He called, "Daddy! Daddy!"

His father groggily answered, "What is it, Andy?"

"I had a bad dream! I'm scared!"

"Just go back to sleep, buddy. It was just a dream."

"But I want you to come and be with me."

Daddy groaned, "Just go back to sleep, Andy. God is with you."

Another brief silence, then, "But I want somebody with skin on!"

"God with skin"—that's an apt way to describe the impact the love of the Christian community can have. There have been times in my life when I could believe no longer myself, but in a very real sense my brothers and sisters were able to believe for me, to hold on to God in my behalf. The New Testament is filled with remarks like this, addressed to suffering, waiting Christians:

Let us consider how we may spur one another on toward love and good deeds. Let us not give up meeting together, as some are in the habit of doing, but let us encourage one another. (Heb 10:24-25)

Acute waiting (and the intense suffering that goes with it) has a way of isolating us. But the time we feel most like running and hiding is the very time we most need to find those who will bear us up as we wait.

There is an old comedian's line about the man who took Carter's Little Liver Pills all of his life. When he died the mortician had to beat his liver to death with a baseball bat. That is what a lifetime spent in close fellowship with God through prayer, the Bible and the worship and fellowship of the church will do. Faith can stay alive in the most acute waiting and trials, even when it seems that just about everything else has died.

Our Isaacs and God's Isaacs

God could not have been more pleased with how Abraham handled this waiting. He said,

> I swear by myself . . . that because you have done this and have not withheld your son, your only son, I will surely bless you and make your descendants as numerous as the stars in the sky and as the sand on the seashore. Your descendants will take possession of the cities of their enemies, and through your offspring all nations on earth will be blessed, because you have obeyed me. (Gen 22:16-18)

The long and short of it was that God would give Abraham all he had promised because Abraham had believed all he had promised when it was most difficult to do so. Abraham had not withheld his one and only son, his beloved Isaac. In letting go of Isaac, he had received him back more fully than he had ever had him before.

165

God has a special affection for those who let go of their Isaacs, their deepest loves, for the sake of a promise. Mount Moriah is very near another mount, perhaps no more than a few hundred yards, that we know as Golgotha. It was there that God gave up his one and only son for the sake of his promise, the very same promise he made to Abraham that day. What Abraham was willing to do, but didn't have to do, God actually did!

Hear this, you who wait, you who struggle to trust God's promises, who have been forced to let go of the things you most love, who strain to believe he is perfect in love, wisdom and power: "He who did not spare his own Son, but gave him up for us all—how will he not also, along with him, graciously give us all things?" (Rom 8:32).

Notes

[1]P. T. Forsyth, *The Soul of Prayer* (Grand Rapids, Mich.: Eerdmans, 1916).
[2]Garrison Keillor, *Leaving Home* (New York: Penguin Books, 1989), p. xxi.

Epilog

Does it strike you as odd that a book on waiting has scarcely mentioned the word *patience?* Or *perseverance?* Aren't those the virtues that we are to exercise when we are forced to wait? They are, but they are secondary to what really is needed to wait with grace. More basic than patience or perseverance are humility and hope. These two are the attitudes, the visions of life, that make patience possible. Patience is a rare and lovely flower that grows only in the soil of humility and hope.

Humility makes patience possible because it shows us our proper place in the universe. God is God, we are his creatures; he is the King, we are his subjects; he is master, we are his servants. We have no demands to make, no rights to assert. I can be impatient only if I think that whatever it is I want is being withheld or delayed unfairly. As Chuck Swindoll put it, "God is not in your appointment book; you're in his." His superiority is not only in power and authority, it is in love and wisdom as well. He has the right to do whatever he wants to do, whenever he wants to do it, but he also has the love to desire what is best for all his creatures and the wisdom to know what is best. He is superior to us in every conceivable way—in power and love and wisdom. To know that is to be patient.

Hope makes patience possible because it gives us the confidence that our wait is not in vain. Hope believes that this God of love, power and wisdom is on our side. It exults in the knowledge that, in the delays of life, he knows exactly what he is doing. If he moves quickly, it is for our good; if he moves slowly, it is for our good. No matter how things look to us, God is the complete master of the situation. There is an old theological word for this—providence. The venerable Heidelberg Catechism defines God's providence as:

> The Almighty and everywhere present power of God; whereby, as it were, by his hand, he upholds and governs heaven, earth, and all creatures; so that herbs and grass, rain and drought, fruitful and barren years, meat and drink, health and sickness, riches and poverty, yea all things come not by chance, but by his fatherly hand.

There are no accidents, no glitches with God. He does all things well. Everything that comes to us comes by his hand and through his heart. He provides for our needs and fulfills our deepest desires in the fullness of time, not a moment too late, nor a second too soon. Hope assures us that in all things, even in the delays of life, God is working for our good. To know that is to be patient.

One of the surprise "goods" that God is working for us as we wait is the forging of our character. What we become as we wait is at least as important as the thing we wait for. To wait in hope is not just to pass the time until the wait is over. It is to see the time passing as part of the process God is using to make us into the people he created us to be. Job emerges from his wait dazzled and transformed. Abram becomes Abraham and Sarai becomes Sarah.

Hope invites us to look at our waitings from the grand perspective of God's eternal purposes. In fact to be a believer is, by definition, to be one who waits. When Jesus won his victory over sin and death, he ascended into heaven, promising one day to return. We Christians wait for that return, poised between the times, in the "already, but not yet." We look back to his victory and strain forward to see its consummation.

The apostle Paul says the pain of our waiting is like the waiting of childbirth. It is the tension and groaning of labor (Rom 8:22-25). I attended my wife in the births of each of our four children. One thing struck me as odd about each event: that the time when she was required to exert her greatest effort and push the baby out was the time when she was least able. She was exhausted from hours of labor and now she was to summon all her strength and push. How could she? Hope made it possible: the hope of giving birth to the child. When human strength was gone, something beyond the purely human took over and gave her the strength she needed.

The Bible said it would be this way for those who hope in God. "Those who hope in the LORD will renew their strength. They will soar on wings like eagles; they will run and not grow weary, they will walk and not be faint" (Is 40:31). Likewise for our Lord Jesus and his cross, "who for the joy set before him endured the cross, scorning its shame, and sat down at the right hand of the throne of God. Consider him . . . so that you will not grow weary and lose heart" (Heb 12:2-3).

My wish is that we might gain the humility and hope to not grow weary and lose heart. I hope that you and I might be able to say, with full hearts, what Henrietta Mears said near the end of her life. This wonderfully eccentric and indefatigable saint accomplished great things for God in her life. When asked if there was anything she would have done differently, had she her life to live over, she said without hesitation, "I would trust God more."